Remembering the Disastrous Battle of Attu Island

****

A Historical Novella Based on the Life of 1st Lieutenant Albert P. Fong, Company F, 2nd Battalion, 17th Infantry, 7th Army Division and the American Army's Pyrrhic Victory over a Tenacious Japanese Garrison on Attu Island in the Aleutian Islands in 1943

Randall L. Got

Published by Low Mon Sing Books
Lake Oswego, Oregon 97034
gots5@aol.com

Printed in the United States of America

First Edition: November 2023

Books and information are available by writing to Low Mon Sing Books at gots5@aol.com.

ALSO BY RANDALL L. GOT

Enlightenment *
A True Story of Life, Love, Interracial Marriage,
the Vietnam War, and Prejudices.

Model Ships of a Septuagenarian
and His Musings About Life, Death and War

54 mm Dioramas of Gangsters,
Pirates, and Gunfighters
of a Septuagenarian and His Musings for 2020

Dioramas of Historical Leaders and
Hollywood Movie Stars, Biographies,
and Critiques on America in 2021

The Analects of **
Low Mon Sing

* Randall L. Got 's Autobiography
** Low Mon Sing is Randall L. Got's
Chinese Name (Cantonese)

Acknowledgment

As an author of six books, I love to write, but I'm an egregiously poor speller because I'm dyslexic. Spell checkers have greatly helped catching my misspellings and typo errors, but does not do a good job in catching improper grammar, pointing out the use of a wrong homophones, or using the wrong tense or verb form. This is why I use a human proofreader to edit my manuscripts who is more than just a spell or grammar checker. He is also a gatekeeper of quality content and insuring that my sentences are engaging, coherent and accurate.

My human proofreader is my cousin Russell Got who has expeditiously and generously spent many hours editing my manuscripts. I can't thank him enough for allocating time from his busy schedule to search for spelling and grammar mistakes in my writings before I can submit my books for publication.

Dedication

I wish to dedicate this book to the so-called "Greatest Generation," also called the "World War II Generation" or the "G.I. Generation," who were born between 1901 and 1924. They came of age during the Great Depression and fought in WWII. Specifically, this dedication is given to the U.S. soldiers who fought on Attu Island back in 1943. Too many of them were killed, wounded, or suffered physical and mental illnesses. And of course, I have to praise my Uncle Albert Fong for his fidelity to his family and to his country.

Table of Contents

Preface

This historical novella is based on the true life of Albert P. Fong who served with the 7th Army Division in World War II and at the Battle of Attu Island, referred to as "The Forgotten Battle." It took place on May 11 to May 30, 1943 between the U.S. 7th Army Division and the Japanese North Sea Garrison. After the bombing of Pearl Harbor, the Japanese wanted a foothold on North American soil and to embarrass the Americans after the Imperial Japanese Navy lost 4 aircraft carriers at the Battle of Midway.

The Story of Albert Paul Fong begins on his graduation day from Springfield College in Springfield, Massachusetts in the summer of 1941. He is a proud second generation American of Chinese heritage who grew up in California and was as American as apple pie on the 4th of July. Albert wanted to show his loyalty to America when he and two of his best college friends, Tony Ricci and Charlie Atwood, who call themselves the "Springfield Musketeers," joined the U.S. Army to do their duty even before the United States was forced into World War II. They were sent to Officer's Candidate School at Fort Benning, Georgia and graduated as 2nd lieutenants.

The newly commissioned 2nd lieutenants were assigned to the 2nd Battalion, 17th Motorized Infantry, 7th Army Division at Fort Ord in California. The 17th was training in desert warfare to fight the Germans in

North Africa should the United States enter into WWII to help Britain defeat Germany and Italy.

When Japan bombed Pearl Harbor on December 7, 1941, the whole world was thrown into turmoil with war on both sides of the world. Now the 17th Infantry Regiment who was training for hot desert warfare was chosen to fight the Japanese on Attu under snowy, cold, foggy, windy, and muddy conditions in the most inhospitable terrain on earth. The American forces sent to retake Attu Island from the Japanese had a 5 to 1 numbers advantage, and a couple of generals predicted that the U.S. Army would defeat the Japanese in 3 days.

Maybe those generals should have listened to Winston Churchill who said, “Never, never, never believe any war will be smooth and easy, or that anyone who embarks on the strange voyage can measure the tides and hurricanes he will encounter. The statesman who yields to fever must realize that once the signal is given, he is no longer the master of policy, but the slave of unforeseeable and uncontrollable events.”

How will the Springfield Musketeers handle the unforeseeable and uncontrollable battles that they will encounter with the Japanese on Attu Island?

Chapter 1
Graduation Day

With the radio playing Kate Smith singing "God Bless America," in the background, the newly graduated Albert P. Fong from Springfield College in Springfield, Massachusetts, Class of 1941, is calling his parents in Vallejo, California to reverberate his joyous milestone of getting his BA in Political Science. "Hello father, how are you and mother doing these days? I'm calling to tell you that I just graduated today, and my buddies Charlie and Tony are going out tonight to celebrate and I want you and mom to be happy for us." His father, Fong Chow, ebulliently replies, "My son, I am so proud of you and with anything you do. Mom, of course wants you to be a professor at U.C. Berkeley so you will be close to home. What are your plans for the future? Your mother and I can hardly wait for you to come back to California. We really miss you." Hesitantly, Albert tells father, "Pop, well I'm not coming home now because Tony, Charlie and I are going to enlist in the Army. You know that Hitler is conquering Europe and is about to defeat England. You said that you will be proud of me in everything that I do, so please understand that I want to do my duty to my country that has given us prosperity and freedom from oppressions like what the Germans and Japanese are doing to the rest of the world. Don't you and mom worry about me. Tony, Charlie, and I are joining up together and we'll help England defeat those Nazis if Roosevelt ever declares war on Germany. I have to run now, but I'll call you after we join up and give you all the details. We're going on Friday to the Springfield recruiting center which is one mile for the campus. Give my love and kisses to my five bossy sisters, big brother Taft, little brother Leslie, and of course to mom. Okay, bye for now!” After Albert hangs up the phone, he hastily changes his clothes and rushes out of his dorm room to meet his fellow graduates down at Lucky's Bar and Grill on 1st Street. When he arrives at the bar, it is full of levity, cold bottles of Hamm's and Schliz beer, and boisterous class mates of '41 cheering the arrival of Albert. He immediately spots his good buddies, Charlie Atwood and Tony Ricci along with their girlfriends, Mary Jo and Carol. They all hug one another and lift their bottles of beer to toast their graduation and their entry into the real world, drowning out the sirens of war in Europe as Germany invades the Soviet Union in June of 1941. Carol hands Albert a bottle of Schilz, but he declines sheepishly saying, “Thanks Carol, but I'm allergic to alcohol which makes my face and whole body to turn red, and I'll vomit if I have more than one beer. I think it is called alcohol flush syndrome.” Charlie chimes in and laughingly says, “I call it the 'Chinese Glow.' Albert is the smartest guy in our class and the nicest person that I know. Plus, I love the guy.” Albert bows to Charlie acknowledging his generous words and then turns to Tony saying, “I know Tony says that alcohol is the social lubricant, easing anxiety and guaranteeing fun, but after I have half a can of beer, he teases me and calls me 'Rudolph the Red-Nose Reindeer.' But don't feel bad for me because you guys know that I don't need any booze to have fun!” This brings a round of laughter from everyone as they continue to celebrate late into the night.

On July 8, 1941, Charlie, Tony, and Albert who now call themselves the “Springfield Musketeers,” sign-up to join the United States Army. Captain Reagan tells the new volunteers to raise their right hand and swear the following, “I (state your name), do solemnly swear that I will support and defend the Constitution of the United States against all enemies, foreign and domestic. I will bear true faith and allegiance to my country; and that I will obey the orders of the President and the orders of the officers appointed over me." He then turns to Albert and says, "Fong, do you know that you are the first American of Chinese ancestry to be inducted at Springfield, Massachusetts? Welcome to the Army."

Because Albert, Charlie, and Tony were college graduates, they were told that they were eligible to be candidates for Officer Candidate School at Fort Benning, Georgia. Albert raises his eyebrows and says, "That sounds good to me. How about you guys?" Charlie thinks, "Well, I guess we were born to be leaders and not followers." Tony replies, "Okay, but only if all of us do it." They all agreed and together they mimic the motto from Alexandre Dumas' 1844 novel, The Three Musketeers, "All for one, one for all." They laugh and shake each others hand.

Captain Reagan hands them pens and sign-up forms, "If you guys just sign these recruitment papers for Officer Candidate School, you will get a notice in the mail on your transportation orders to Fort Benning, Georgia." After they fill out and sign the forms, Albert shakes Captain Reagan's hand, "Thank you sir, I really don't believe what happened." Tony says," Hey, let's get the girls and tell them what we just did. They are going to freak out."

At the girl's dormitory, the guys call out for Mary Jo and Carol. As the girls sign out of the dorms, they gather around a picnic table on the front lawn and Mary Jo says, "Why do you guys have those funny grins? What did you guys just do?" Charlie looks at Carol and kisses Mary Jo, "Well, you pretty little things, We just signed up for Officer Candidate School and we'll be going to Fort Benning, Georgia." A surprised Mary Jo reacts, "Why did you guys do that? Isn't the Army commitment for an officer 6 years? Non commissioned officers are for only 4 years. I'm going to be an old maid by the time you get out of the Army. Oh, I'm so mad at you." "Don't be upset, it is only two more years, and then we will be together forever." "I'm not so sure. You are always looking at pretty girls and you'll probably hook up with some Fräulein or some French bimbo." "You know I just look, you are the only one for me." Albert steps in saying, "Mary Jo, officers have better lives in the Army than NCO's. Rank has privileges and you could probably come and stay with him no matter where he is stationed." A calm Mary Jo looks at Charlie, "Is that true Charlie?" "Sure honey, you should be able to stay wherever I get stationed as long as we don't have to go to war over in Europe." Charlie and Mary Jo hug and kiss each other. Tony interrupts, "Okay everyone let's go down to Lucky's and get a hamburger and milk shake."

The following week the Springfield Musketeers got their transportation orders to fly to Fort Benning for the 12-week Officer Candidate School. When they arrived at the induction station for the class of '41, Major General Williamson addressed the class of 50 cadets with these welcoming words, "Congratulations on your selection for officer candidate training. It is highly admirable that you chose to pursue a commission and serve your country as a member of its corps. As you know, Fort Benning, Georgia is 'Home of the Infantry' and its mission is to train and commission 2nd lieutenants for the Army. A competent cadre will train you on the fundamentals of leadership and basic military skills, instill Army values and officership, and lastly evaluate your leadership potential. We will commission only those who meet the challenge and succeed."

The next day dressed in their fatigues, the cadets reported down to the company PT field for Basic Combat

Training. Here they were greeted by Major Johnston and welcomed them to the toughest training school in the United States Army. “Standing beside me is First Sergeant Willie Savage and he will be in charge of your physical training sessions and you will not be treated as officers, because you are not yet commissioned. Before you can give orders, you first have to learn how to take orders. He will not baby you and will use unkind words if you screw up. Remember if you do not past this Basic Combat course, you will be eliminated from moving on to the Advanced Combat Training classes. Sergeant Savage will now instruct you in PT physical training this morning.” “Alright men, spread out in five rows of 10 and give me 25 jumping jacks.” “Okay, now give me 25 push-ups.” “Very good, now 25 sit-ups.” “I see that some of you are going to have to bulk up and eat a lot less ice cream. Now follow me over to the oval track and we'll do a mile run.” When the mile run was over, several of the men were way behind walking slowly and out of breath to the disgust of Sergeant Savage, “If you girls don't start running, you'll have to do another lap,”

On the first week, the cadets spent three days at the M1 Mechanical Training course. Sergeant Savage yells out, “Not only will you learn how to fire a M1 rifle with keen accuracy, you are going to know how to clean, take apart and put it back together again.” Albert is all fired up to shoot the M1 because he has never held a gun or rifle in his life. “I've never fired a gun or rifle.” Tony who is next to Albert says, “I'll help you, I know all about rifles, my dad was an avid deer hunter and on my tenth birthday, he took me deer hunting for the first time. I shot one, but after I killed it, I felt really bad and cried.” Cadet Swanson next to Charlie asked a question about the M1 to Sergeant Savage, “Hey Sarg, how much does this gun weigh?" "Hey retard-brain that is the second time you called the M1 rifle a gun. So that you will remember the difference between a rifle and a gun, I want you to take your rifle and run around the PT field two times." "Yes, Sarg." "Oh, and when you get there I want you to unzipper your fatigue trouser and hold onto your ding-dong in your left hand and your M1 rifle in your right hand and sing this instructive couplet while you are running. 'This is my rifle and this is my gun, one for fighting and one is for fun.' Get over there now!"

The following week the class went to the hand grenade range and Master Sergeant Hector Sanchez was the instructor in charge. "Hello Class of '41, today you will learn to blow those Nazis back to Kingdom Come. When it is your turn to throw the hand grenade, you will be handed a grenade and place it in your throwing hand. There are five steps to learn before throwing your grenade. One, locate your target before you ready your grenade. Don't even grab your grenade until you've identified an enemy position you intend to strike. Two, grip the grenade in the palm of your hand with the pull ring pointing up. Use your thumb to put steady pressure on the safety metal lever running from the top down the side of the grenade. Three, pull the pin with your non-throwing index finger. Four, throw with an overhand motion, the same way as a baseball. And five, take cover and lie prone behind any available cover to protect yourself from shrapnel. You'll have about four to five seconds before the grenade detonates."

When it came time for Albert's turn to throw a grenade Master Sergeant Sanchez said, "Fong which hand is your throwing hand?" "My right." "Put your left index finger in the ring and pull it out, and throw that Nazi killer as far as you can." "Bombs away!" Fong and Sanchez ducked behind the protective wall. Five, ten seconds goes by, but there is no explosion. “Shit Fong, did you pull the rin out of the grenade?” “Yes I did, see I have the ring on my finger” “Yah, but the ring opened up and didn't pull the safety pin out to release the safety lever to ignite the fuse to the explosive charge. You had a defective grenade.” “Do I get to throw another grenade?” “No Fong, only one grenade per cadet.” “Damn, I want to throw a real working grenade.” “Next cadet.”

On week four, the class was sent down to the Bayonet Assault Course under the guidance of Drill Sergeant Leonard Henley, “In close combat warfare and hand to hand fighting the bayonet is your best friend when you run out of bullets. A clean and sharp bayonet could save your life, so don't lose it and take care of it just like you would your girlfriend.” The class took out their bayonets and mounted it on their rifles. “Take a step forward and thrust your rifle forward at the same time. Now each of you run down the Assault Course and stab the hay stacks at each target location. And as you stab each hay stack, think it is a Nazi or maybe a guy who is stealing your girl while you are fighting for your country.” When the cadets finished the bayonet training, they were sent on a one mile run with their M1 rifles at a double time pace. They were then ordered to hold their rifles over their head for several minutes at a time. The run was lead by Captain Andy McDay who had the men sing motivating jingles as they ran in the boiling sun:

“I want to be an Army ranger, I want to live a life of danger, here we go Army, here we go, here go Army, here we go. I want to be an Army ranger, I want to live a life of danger, all the way Army, all the way. All the way Army, all the way!”

Then Captain McDay sang another jingle which the men cheerfully followed along singing:

"Around her hair, she wore a yellow ribbon. She wore her yellow ribbon, in the merry month of May. And if, you asked her, why the heck she wore it? She wore it, for her trooper boy, far, far away. Far awaay, far awaay. She wore it, for her trooper boy, far, far away."

Sadly, two of the cadets had to stop and fell to the ground while dropping their rifles. Behind those fallen cadets, were Charlie, Albert, and Tony running together. Along with another cadet, they stopped to help lift those exhausted cadets up. As the other cadets ran on, the Springfield Musketeers and a wannabe d'Artagnan helped to support and walk the two sun-stricken cadets back to camp. Charlie and Tony also carried the rifles of the weaken cadets as well as their own.

Over the first 6 weeks, the cadets had classes in M1 Mechanical Training, Bayonet, Trainfire, Target Detection, Record Firing, Hand Grenade, Pugil Stick, Hand to Hand Combat, Individual Tactical Training, Combat Firing, and First Aid sessions. On the last day of the Physical Training Sessions, they had to run a mile for time, and had to take a written test to rate their proficiency. Those who made the grade, moved on to the 6-week Advance Officer Training Sessions. Cadets Fong. Atwood, and Ricci passed with flying colors along with 38 other cadets, 9 were disqualified and sent home.

Over the next six weeks of AOTS, the cadets were taught and learned about Leadership Principals, Military Intelligence, Battle Drills, Map Reading, Navigation, Applied Field Exercises, Communication Skills, and Military History. The weeks quickly passed and on October 20, 1941, Cadets Fong, Ricci, Atwood, and 32 others were awarded the commission of second lieutenant. Six cadets failed because of ill health or poor test scores.

Chapter 2
California Here We Come

As the newly commissioned 2nd lieutenants awaited their orders for their station assignments from the Levy Department, they were fitted for their new officer's uniforms. When the assignment orders were issued, seven of the lieutenants were to be sent to Fort Ord in Monterey, California. They were lieutenants Miller, Pickett, Fong, Milo, Ricci, Taylor, and Atwood, and were assigned to the 17th Motorized Infantry Regiment, 7th Army Division. The insignia of the 7th Division consists of two black, equilateral triangles placed vertically on a red circular disc, with their apexes in juxtaposition at the center of the disc. The similarity of the double triangles to an hourglass was responsible for the nickname, "Hour-Glass Division." After all of the assignments were issued, the Fort Ord lieutenants met in the dining hall for dinner to celebrate their commission and assignment to sunny California.

Lieutenant Robert A. Miller who planned the dinner party asked his fellow lieutenants to lift their wine glasses filled with a fine Cabernet and makes a toast, "To seven sex-crazy beer sucking college grads who are now seven officers and gentlemen. Hoo-Rah!" All seven lieutenants stand up and repeat, "Hoo-Rah, Hoo-Rah!" Lieutenant Frank Milo takes over, "I can't believe we lucked out and got stationed at Fort Ord, sunny California. I've never been there and I hear the girls are gorgeous out there. Is anyone here from California? Albert is the only one raising his hand, "I guess that I'm the only one from California." Milo asks, "What city did you grow-up in?" "I was born in a small gold-mining town in Northern California called 'Washington,' and when I was two years old, my family moved down to Vallejo which is about 30 miles from San Francisco." Lieutenant Ken Taylor asks, "Do you have any brothers or sisters?" "I have five sisters and two brothers." "Wow, you have a large family, I don't have any siblings." "I had a brother Theodore who was named after Theodore Roosevelt, but he died before I was born." "I'm sorry to hear that. What happened to him?" "My dad doesn't like to talk about it, but in 1915 when Theodore was twelve years old, dad sent him to China to visit our grandfather, grandmother, aunts and uncles. Shortly after he got there he was kidnapped by Chinese Bandits and they demanded a ransom of twenty-five thousand dollars in American Gold Eagle coins. The ransom was never paid because dad didn't have close to that amount of money, so the bandits beat and killed Theodore. My dad felt so guilty and responsible for his death that he vowed never to go back to China again." Tony remarks, "Gee Albert, you never told me about Theodore." "Well, I haven't told hardly anyone about him." Lieutenant Jay Pickett remarks, "Fong, I'm from Louisiana and I've never met a Chinese person before I met you, and you're as American as apple pie. The only Chinese I knew about were 'Ming the Merciless' in the Flash Gordon TV serials and Charlie Chan movies. You don't talk like them" "That's because I'm a second generation American, Jay." "Oh, I loved those Flash Gordon Serials" "Ming the Merciless sure gave the Chinese a bad name, and he even wasn't Chinese. I think the actor's name is Charles Middleton."

Albert wants to change the subject, "Hey, you guys are going to love California. Fort Ord is located in Monterey on the edge of Monterey Bay. San Francisco is a wonderful city with its cable cars, fisherman's wharf, fabulous restaurants, the Golden Gate Bridge, Golden Gate Park, and the biggest Chinatown in America. My dad owns an apartment building near there on Powell street. In Northern California is the most beautiful Alpine lake called Lake Tahoe, and there are a couple of casinos on the Nevada side of the lake. Southern California has great beaches and Hollywood movie stars. After I get out of the Army, I plan to live in California for the rest of my life."

The following week, with newly pressed uniforms with a shiny gold bar on each of their shoulders, the seven 2nd lieutenants were taken over to the Fort Benning airfield and flown to the airfield at Fort Ord, California. After they landed, they were trucked over to the Officer's Quarters Mess barrack at building T-1024, and shown to their rooms. After they were all settled in, they walked over to building T-1044 which was the headquarters of the 7th Division Headquarters and reported in. They were told to report to Captain Butler down the hall who handles incoming transfers. Lieutenant Ricci was the first to enter Captain Butler's office followed by Fong and Atwood, "Captain Butler, we just arrived from Fort Benning and reporting in with our transfer orders." "Welcome lieutenants, we were expecting you and needing new officers to strengthen the ranks of the 17th Regiment." "Sir, we were overjoyed to learn that we were assigned to the 17th here at Ford Ord, and eager to learn which battalion we will be assigned to." "I'm pleased to hear that. Let me process your transfer orders and then you can report to your Commanding Officer Major Edwin Smith of the 2nd Battalion, and he will decide what battalion and company you men will be assigned to." "Thank you sir." After they were processed in, they were taken over to the 2nd Battalion headquarters to see Commanding Officer Major Smith in building T-1045. Major Smith greets the three 2nd lieutenants, "Gentlemen, I heard that you all arrived safely and anxious to know which battalion I'm assigning you to. As you know the 7th Division is under the command of General Joseph W. Stilwell and the 17th regiment has been training for desert warfare if the United States is ever forced into war against Germany and Italy. The 17th regiment if called upon, is to assist the British in North Africa to defeat Germany's Colonel General Erwin Rommel and his famous Panzerarmee Afrika with their Panzer IV tanks. Our Regiment has been training in the Mojave Desert for the last month. We will be ready to go overseas when called upon. I have assigned you to Company F of the 2nd Battalion and your commanding officer is Captain Delbert L. Bjork. He is a fine officer and tough as nails. I understand that you have 7-day passes to visit your families back home. When you return off leave, you and Lieutenants Milo, Miller, Pickett, and Taylor will be sent to the Mojave Desert to join your battalion. Until then, you'll be free to visit the beautiful towns of Monterey and Carmel and rest up from your long flight from Georgia. That's all for now." They salute Major Smith, "Thank you sir."

As the Springfield Musketeers walked back to their barrack, Albert suggests, "Hey guys, I've been to Monterey before and they have a couple of good seafood restaurants down by the wharf. I'll show you their famous Cannery Row and all of the sardines that they process. Then there is a little town called Carmel overlooking a white sand beach that you have to see." Tony says, "That sounds good to me. Let's go over to the motor pool and borrow a Jeep."

The next day, Charlie got on a plane to fly to Chicago to see his family, and Tony got on another plane and flew to Houston to see his family and girl friend. Albert didn't have to fly home because Vallejo was only 160 miles away from Fort Ord. So he borrowed an Army jeep and drove home. When Albert drove over the Carquinez

Bridge which connects interstate 80 between Crockett and Vallejo, California, his heart swelled with anticipated joy in seeing his family. It was only another three miles to reach his home on Georgia street. His father who was an immigrant from China who moved his large family of nine from the California Gold Country to Vallejo in 1916 and built a successful grocery business. The Fong family would be know as a "family of firsts," in Vallejo. Sister Alice was the first Chinese-American teacher in the San Francisco Public School system. Sister Martha was the first nursery school teacher of Chinese ancestry. Sister Minnie was the first Chinese-American public health nurse and sister Marian was the first Chinese-American dental hygienist.

With such a talented pool of sisters, Albert felt a lot of pressure to be recognized and to show that he was special too. This motivated him to be a true officer and gentleman, strong in leadership, respected as well as respectful. Courageous, but not rash. Wise, but not full of hubris. And to be the "first officer" to lead his men on the field of battle.

As Albert pulled his jeep into the family driveway, his sister Marian, who is two years younger, was the first out the door to hug and squeeze her handsome big brother. Albert shouts, "How have you been? It's been over two years since I've been home. I hear that you were a showgirl at the 'Forbidden City' nightclub in San Francisco. Bet mom and dad didn't approve of you dancing there." "Well, I'm a dental hygienist now cleaning people's teeth. Not as much fun as dancing, but more respectable in the Chinese community." Next to empty the house were mom, dad, Alice, Taft, Leslie, Helen, and Martha followed by Suzy the family dog. Minnie was overseas with her husband Ira on business, so most of the family was there to celebrate with Albert over the next six days. At the family dinner table mother prepared the most fancy dishes which included lotus root soup, black bean spareribs, family style bean curd, Chinese mixed green vegetables with black mushrooms, and Albert's favorite, sweet and sour pig's feet made with Chinese brown sugar, red vinegar, and lots of ginger. Father asked Albert about the Army's war preparations if America has to got to war, “Since I just got to Fort Ord, I don't know too much except that my regiment is training for desert warfare and I'll be training in the Mojave Desert when I get back to the fort. Major Smith says that if we do go to war with Germany, we will be sent to North Africa to fight General Rommel's Africa Corp.” “The German's are powerful enemies and I'm worried that you and many of your men may not make it back home.” “Don't you and mom worry, our military has been preparing for war and our regiment is going to give them Hell.” Younger sister Martha wants to change the conversational mood and talk about Albert's personal life and asks, “Hey, Albee, have you found a girl friend yet? I bet there lots of pretty army nurses at Fort Ord.” “Well there are, but none of them are Chinese.” “Hey, silly, White girls know how to kiss too.” “Baby sister, you could be right, but a soldier going off to war isn't high on a girl's list looking for a boyfriend. I'll tell you what though, when I get out of the army, I promise you that I'll find some lovely girl to marry and have many kids. Mom, how many grandchildren do you and dad want?”

Over the next six days, mother and father Fong still had to work at their busy grocery store. Albert spent the week playing tennis with his sisters, visiting an old high school friend, playing chess with Taft, and reading the Vallejo Times newspaper for the latest geopolitical and war news stories. Although Albert was happy being at home with his family, his mind was never free of the thoughts of going to war and his responsibilities of watching over the safety of his men that would be u his command.

When Albert's 7-day pass was about to expire, he hugged his family good-bye and very slowly got into his jeep and drove away. On the three hour drive back to Fort Ord, he eagerly tried to polish up on his German so that he could interrogate any captured Nazi soldiers. He practices:

"Zu weichem regiment gehorst du?" (What regiment do you belong to?).

'Wie heilst der General?" (What is your general's name?).

"Magst du Hitler wirklich?" (Do you really like Hitler?)

"Wie viele Amerikaner solaten haben sie erschossen?" (How many American soldiers have you shot?)

Mogen Deutsche chinesisches essen? (Do Germans like Chinese food?)

When Albert got back to Fort Ord, he was ready to rolled up his sleeves to get ready for training in the heat of the Mojave Desert. But first he was glad to see his good buddies and fellow lieutenants Charlie and Tony. "Hey, I see you guys made it home and back safely. I hope you had a good time with your loved ones like I did with my family?" Charlie replies, "When I got home my mother told me that she had stage-4 breast cancer and that she had maybe only 12-16 months to live. My dad is a plumber, but he will only be able to work part-time now because he will have to take care of mom. He is in a really shitty predicament." Tony hugs Charlie and says,

"Hey man, I'm sorry to hear that your mother has cancer. I never knew my mother because she ran away when I was two years old and she never came back. My dad remarried a woman who never liked me, so we never got along." Albert replies, "Gee, you never told me about your mother and step-mother. That's so sad. By the way, how was your time with Carol? Are you guys still planning to get married next year?" With a glowing smile on Tony's face, he says, "We sure are! Her parents are planning for a huge church wedding and you are going to be my best man!" "What? A best man has to give a speech and say wonderful things about you. Hell, I truly can't think of one good thing that you have done." All three of them, fill the room with laughter.

A week later, Major Smith, his staff and the newly assigned 2nd lieutenants to the 2nd Battalion boarded a plane and flew down to the Mojave Desert which is one of the smallest and driest deserts of North American deserts. It is also referred to as the "High Desert" because most of it is 2,000 to 4,000 feet above sea level. In the northern part of the desert lies Death Valley which is 282 feet below sea level. Back in 1913, it reached a temperature of 134 °F. The plane landed at the training camp that was set up in 1940 to train U.S. soldiers in desert warfare, and the use of anti-aircraft weapons and artillery. Greeting the plane was Colonel T.J. Rogers the commanding officer, "Good to see you again Major Smith." "Likewise Colonel Rogers. I like you to meet lieutenants, Taylor, Miller, Atwood, Fong, Ricci, Milo and Pickett." "Welcome gentlemen to one of the hottest places on earth. The 2nd Battalion will complete their training in about two weeks, so you men will not have to suffer in this 102 temperature for a very long time and then the 2nd Battalion will be sent back to Fort Ord. Let's get into some Jeeps and drive over to where your battalion is training and introduce you to Captain Robert Edwards and the men of the 2nd Battalion." "

After a short drive over the vast expanse of sand, they arrive to the sounds of rifle and artillery fire and a field of hundreds of soldiers practicing attack maneuvers. Colonel Rogers gets off the lead Jeep and greets Major Standeven, "Good afternoon Elan, I brought you seven lieutenants to help bolster your battalion." "Great, I'll have them sent over to meet the CO's of companies E, F, G, and H for their assignments. Let's come into my tent and get out of this sun. I've got some classified information to tell you."

Sergeant First Class Mackin drove the new lieutenants Milo and Taylor over to H company, lieutenant Pickett to G company, lieutenant Miller to E company, and lieutenants Fong, Ricci, and Atwood to F company. The CO of F company, Captain Delbert L. Bjork, greets the new lieutenants. "Hello gentlemen, what are your names?" "I'm Lieutenant Fong, sir." "I'm Lieutenant Atwood, sir." "and I'm Lieutenant Ricci, sir." "Well welcome to company F. Do you know what company F stands for?" No, sir" "It stands for First, Fit, and Fearsome. After the men finish their training for today, I will have a dinner meeting so you can meet the other lieutenants of the our company. Lets get into some covered vehicles and I'll show you around. Sergeant Manley get us a couple of M151 jeeps with overhead covers." "Yes Sir."

Meeting for dinner at the company mess tent, the new lieutenants are introduced to Lieutenants Hahn, Reynolds, and Brundage. All the lieutenants will be platoon leaders. F company's platoons consisted of a 1st or 2nd lieutenant, a platoon sergeant and four squads of 12 men.

During the next week the regiment trained in driving and transporting infantry in trucks, and other non-armored motor vehicles to allow soldiers to move faster to critical sectors of the battlefield, to outmaneuver the enemy, and to respond to enemy movements. The disadvantages are that they are vulnerable to artillery and small arms fire. They also learned how to keep hydrated and to protect themselves from getting sun-stroke from the blistering heat of the Mojave Desert. The last week of training quickly passed, and the 17th Motorized Infantry Regiment was flown back to Fort Ord. When the Springfield Musketeers got back to Fort Ord on December 4, 1941 they were joyous to breathe the cool and misty air of Monterey. With Christmas only 21 days away, they anxiously looked forward to the holiday season and the coming New Year. Albert tells Charlie and Tony, "let's go down to the commissary and buy some Christmas gift for our families. I know my family really celebrates Christmas. They always cut down a tree and decorate it with strings of lights, bulbs, and tinsel. They pick names to see who they have to buy a present for, but they don't tell who it is from. Like a secret Santa. On Christmas morning they have a big breakfast, then sing Christmas carols, and open the presents. Oh, how I'm going to miss that." Tony comments, "My step mother is Jewish and my father is a Christian. They alternate years putting up a Christmas tree and the following year they don't. On the years they don't celebrate Christmas, on the 25th of December they go out and eat Chinese food and go out to a movie." Charlie says, "My parents love Christmas because it is the celebration of Jesus' birth and they shun any association with Santa, but I don't so lets go and buy some presents for our families." However, their holiday and Christmas plans were crushed three days later when the Empire of Japan surreptitiously bombed Pearl Harbor.

Chapter 3
America Goes To War

On the early morning of December 7, 1941, the Empire of Japan bombed Pearl Harbor, killing 2,393 sailors, soldiers, marines, and civilians. They also wounded 1,178 military personnel and civilians. Losses included 4 battleships sunk, 4 battleships damaged, 3 light cruisers damaged, 3 destroyers damaged, 1 harbor tug sunk, 188 aircraft destroyed, and 159 aircraft damaged.

On hearing about this devastating and dastardly news, Charlie rushed over to find Albert and Tony in their barrack and shouted, "The Japs just bombed Pearl Harbor and oh my God, we are going to war with them." Tony who was more agitated than Charlie swore out, "Those damn yellow monkeys are going burn in Hell after we blow them to bits." But Albert just scratched this head and said to the guys, "Hey, we aren't going to shoot any of them because we will be going to Europe to kill Krauts!" Tony angrily replies, "You are probably right, but after we kill all those Nazis bastards, I hope the Army sends us over the to the Pacific to kill those sneaky Japs for bombing Pearl!"

The next morning the 2nd Battalion was called together for a general assembly to hear President Franklin Roosevelt's radio message to the nation about the attack on Pearl Harbor and to ask Congress to declare war.

"Mr. Vice President, Mr. Speaker, Members of the Senate, and of the House of Representatives: Yesterday, December 7th, 1941- a date which will live in infamy- The United States of America was suddenly and deliberately attacked by naval and air forces of the Empire of Japan. The United States was at peace with that nation and, at the solicitation of Japan, was still in conversation with its government and its emperor looking toward the maintenance of peace in the Pacific.

Indeed, one hour after Japanese air squadrons had commenced bombing in the American island of Oahu, the Japanese ambassador to the United States and his colleague delivered to our Secretary of State a formal reply to a recent American message. And while this reply stated that it seemed useless to continue the existing diplomatic negotiations, it contained no threat or hint of war or of armed attack.

It will be recorded that the distance of Hawaii from Japan makes it obvious that the attack was deliberately planned many days or even weeks ago. During the intervening time, the Japanese government has deliberately sought to deceive the United States by false statements and expressions of hope for continued peace.

The attack yesterday on the Hawaiian islands has caused severe damage to American naval and military forces. I regret to tell you that very many American lives have been lost. In addition, American ships have been reported torpedoed on the high seas between San Francisco and Honolulu. Yesterday, the Japanese government also launched an attack against Malaya. Last night, Japanese forces attacked Hong Kong. Last night, Japanese forces attacked Guam. Last night, Japanese forces attacked the Philippine Islands. Last night, the Japanese attacked Wake Island. And this morning, the Japanese attacked Midway Island.

Japan has, therefore, undertaken a surprise offensive extending throughout the Pacific area. The facts of yesterday and today speak for themselves. The people of the United States have already formed their opinions and well understand the implications to the very life and safety of our nation. As commander in Chief of the Army and Navy, I have directed that all measures be taken for our defense. But always will our whole nation remember the character of the onslaught against us.

No matter how long, it may take us to overcome this premeditated invasion, the American people in their righteous might will win through to absolute victory. I believe that I interpret the will of the Congress and of the people when I assert that we will not only defend ourselves to the uttermost, but will make it very certain that this form of treachery shall never again endanger us. Hostilities exist. There is no blinking at the fact that our people, our territory, and our interests are in grave danger.

With confidence in our armed forces, with the unbounding determination of our people, we will gain the inevitable triumph-so help us God. I ask that the Congress declare that since the unprovoked and dastardly attack by Japan on Sunday, December 7th, 1941, a state of war has existed between the United States and the Japanese Empire."

Three days after having declared war against Japan, Congress also voted to declare war against Nazi Germany and Fascist-ruled Italy. This was because Germany and Italy were allies of Japan, prompting Adolf Hitler, during a speech to the Reichstag in Berlin, to declare war on the United States. Much to the regret of Italy, it did the same. After war was declared on the Axis Powers, the 2nd Battalion quickly received their hastily assembled plans for real war against Germany. The officers worked night and day for several weeks to coordinate and implement directives from the Department of War and from General Dwight D. Eisenhower who was appointed supreme American General of the European theater when the United States of America was bombed into World War II.

Chapter 4
Waiting to Fight the Germans

Since the 17th, 23rd, and the 159th (a California National Guard Unit) Infantry Regiments, 7th Army Division was at Fort Ord, California, it was ordered to patrol the coasts of California, Oregon, and Washington to allay the local populace's fear of a Japanese invasion. This delayed the 7th Army Division from being deployed to North Africa. Captain Bjork was upset over the delay and told his lieutenants so, “I think we are wasting out time preparing to protect the West Coast from a Japanese invasion. I know the Japs are crazy, but not that crazy to want to invade the Western States of America. I heard some intelligence officers say that Japan would not invade us because they knew that almost every American had guns in their homes and that they knew how to use them. Lieutenant Fong replies, “I think the Japanese would not seriously want to invade the West Coast because there is the Pacific Ocean between us and logistically it's not doable. Lieutenant Reynolds agrees, “The West Coast is safe from invasion, but Alaska is possible which is half way between here and Japan.” Lieutenant Ricci comments, “I agree with everyone. I hope the War Department sees it too and send us to North Africa. I can't wait to shoot some Krauts.”

With Christmas fast approaching, the Springfield Musketeers are looking forward to the Christmas Eve dance at the Officer's Club with the Fort Ord nurses. On the evening of the 24th, Albert, Tony and Charlie all sharp-looking in their Army dress uniforms enter the Officer's Club to the music of the Fort Ord's dance band. They find a table by the dance floor perusing the nurses as the band plays “Moonlight Serenade.” Charlie is quick to spot a table with three nurses, “Hey guys, let's go over there and introduce ourselves to those three lovely ladies.” Tony says, “Lead the way point man.” Charlie introduces himself to the nurses, “Good evening ladies, my name is Charlie Atwood and these good-looking gentlemen are my good friends Tony Ricci and Albert Fong. May I inquire as to your lovely names?” The blond nurse smiles and introduces herself and her friends. “I'm Nan Frazier, and this is Shawn Wilson and Judee Chung” “And will you ladies do us the honor of having our first dance tonight with us?” “We most certainly will.” Charlie pairs up with Nan, Tony with Shawn, and Albert with Judee. After the music stops, the three nurses are escorted back to their table and the Three Musketeers thank the ladies for the dance and excuse themselves as they head towards the bar. Tony comments, “Shawn was a great dancer and not bad looking, but I'm engaged to Carol, so I don't want to get involved with another gal.” Charlie concurs, “Yeah, me too. I promised Mary Jo that I would be true to her, so I'm just going to have a couple of “stingers,” talk to the guys, and listen to the big band music.” Albert speaks up, “I think that Judee likes me. She whispered into my ear and said that I was a very smooth dancer. Should I ask her for another dance?” Tony smiles, “Albert, you need to hook up with some gal. You don't want to go through life all alone do you? You need to loosen-up and take a chance on love.” “I'm going to ask her for another dance. Wish me good luck.” Albert asks Judee for another dance and they danced the night away to songs like “In a Sentimental Mood,” “The way you look tonight,” and “You made me love you.” At the end of the night Judee gives Albert her hospital unit's telephone number and kisses him goodnight and tells him, “Santa brought me an early Christmas present.” Albert walked back to the barracks on “cloud nine” and couldn't wait to tell Tony and Charlie that he has been smitten by Judee Chung.

The men of the 7th Army Division at Fort Ord spent the next six months continuing desert warfare training and adjusting tactical maneuvers based on how well the British were fairing against the Germans in the Libyan and Egyptian deserts and in Morocco and Algeria as well. The British North African campaign started in June of 1940 and the United States just started to send direct military assistance in May of 1942.

On the other side of the world the Japanese were planning to attack the Midway Atoll which is strategically placed in the Pacific Ocean for both sides to further their operations in the region. In late May, a Japanese Naval task force departed Japan to attack Midway. However, they sent a diversionary force pretending to invade the Attu and Kiska Islands hoping to draw the American carriers out of Pearl to intercept the fake invasion of the Aleutian Islands. Fortunately, the American code breakers learned of the Japanese plan to attack Midway and secretly formed a naval task force of their own of three aircraft carriers, the USS Enterprise, USS Yorktown, and USS Hornet. The Japanese Midway task force was made up of four aircraft carriers the IJN Akagi, Kaga, Soryu, and Kiryu along with the largest battleship ever built the IJN Yamato.

In the early morning hours of June 4, 1942, Japanese Vice Admiral Nagumo launched over 100 fighters and bombers against Midway. The American fighter planes on Midway were launched to engage the Japanese planes. Soon after the USS Hornet and the USS Enterprise launched 151 aircraft and when sightings of the American planes coming to attack the Japanese fleet, a surprised Admiral Nagumo immediately recalled his Mitsubishi "Zero" fighter planes to defend the carriers.

The Yamato Battleship stayed 300 miles behind its carriers and was not threatened by the American fighters. The USS Yorktown soon launched it's fighters and bombers against the Japanese carriers. Within a short time, the IJN Akagi, Kaga, and Soryu were sinking from American bombs. The IJN Hiryu was a mile away from her three sinking carriers and launched her bombers and fighters against the USS Yorktown. The IJN Hiryu was soon sunk as well. As the USS Yorktown was recovering her aircraft, she took three direct hits, but did not sink. Her crew was transferred to other ships and days later as the USS Yorktown was being towed, she was torpedoed by a Japanese submarine and sunk.

By the end of the Battle of Midway, the Japanese Navy was effectively crippled and not a force to be reckoned with for the rest of the war. Not only did she lose four aircraft carriers, she loss thousands of personnel, irreplaceable airmen and aircraft. She also loss the use of the Battleship Yamato because she could not sail because she needed aircraft carriers to defend herself. The dominance of aircraft carriers could easily sink any battleship even with nine 18 inch guns.

****

The Japanese defeat at Midway did not discourage them from attacking the Aleutians Islands in which two Japanese aircraft carriers launched air strikes against Army and Navy facilities on Amknak Island. Their attack did not draw the American Naval forces away from Midway as they hoped it would. On June 3, 1942, they attacked Dutch Harbor with 62 light bombers and fighters. Next the Japanese landed their 3rd Navy Landing Force and a 750-man construction company on Kiska Island. They started to bring in anti-aircraft guns, aircraft and midget submarines turning Kiska into their major foothold in American territory. At the same time, Major Matsutoshi Hozumi landed at Holtz Bay, Attu Island, with the 1,143-man North Sea Detachment, consisting of the 301st Independent Infantry Battalion and the 301st Engineer Company. The next day the Japanese crossed over the difficult snow-covered Holtz Bay-Chichagof Harbor Pass and entered into Attu Village occupied by 43 Aleuts. After raising the Japanese flag, they allowed the Aleuts to remain in the village.

When the Japanese invaded the Aleutian Islands, it was the first time since the War of 1812 that a Foreign Power landed on and occupied an American Territory. On June 11, 1942 the Eleventh Army Air Force flew B-24 Liberator bombers from Cape Field on Umnak Island to bombard Kiska which was 620 miles to the west. They loss a B-24 and its crew on the first mission and the Navy loss a PBY and its crew on the final mission on June the 14th. The bombing and loss of two planes and 19 Americans had no effect on driving the Japanese from Kiska.

Instead, the military decided to place American forces on unoccupied Adak Island on August 30, 1942. They built a 5,000-foot runway and airfield within 10 days for bombers and fighters putting them within 250 air miles of Kiska and 442 air miles from Attu. On September 14, 1942, the Eleventh Army Air Force launched its first raid of 40 bombers and fighters on Kiska Island. Adak now became the major headquarters base for the Army and Navy in the North Pacific.

With the American presence in the eastern Aleutians and their threat to Japan, the Japanese decided to increase their strongholds on Kiska and Attu Island and moved the garrison on Attu to Kiska. They also planned to send a replacement garrison to Attu Island at a future date. Of the 43 Aleuts on Attu, one died of natural causes, while the rest were sent to Japan on September 17, 1942. The Japanese reoccupied Attu Island on October 29, 1942 with 500 men under the command of Lieutenant Colonel Hiroshi Yonekawa. It consisted of an under-strength infantry battalion and an engineering unit.

By January 1943, the Americans increased their blockade of Japanese cargo ships. On January 6th, bombing crews sank the Kotohiro Maru off Holtz Bay, Attu bringing in a load of provisions, fuel and building materials. The very next day, another bombing crew sank the Montreal Maru heading towards Kiska with a cargo of airfield construction materials and a contingent of engineers. Bad weather, in addition to the increased American blockade, force the Japanese to cancel further cargo and troop shipments through the month of February.

In March of 1943, the weather improved and the Japanese resumed cargo shipments to Kiska and Attu with an escort of four warships. March 11th was the last time Japanese surface ships were able to resupply the islands with anti-aircraft guns, ammunition, and airfield construction materials. Submarines were now the only way for the Japanese to transport supplies and men between Attu and Kiska, and their support bases in the Northern Kuril Islands about 800 miles from Hokkaido in Japan. On March 18th, a submarine carrying troops and Colonel Yasuyo Yamazaki landed on Attu Island increasing the Japanese garrison to 2,650 men. Under Yamazaki's command the Japanese increased their strongholds high in the mountains, trenches, and ridges. They built snow covered machine gun nests, and anti-aircraft installations in the high grounds in preparation of an imminent attack from the Americans. Most of the men were from Hokkaido who liked cold weather. They were not going to be easily defeated.

Chapter 5
Decision to Retake Attu Island

Back at Fort Ord, California the 2nd Battalion, 17th Infantry Regiment, 7th Army Division was still waiting for their orders to go to North Africa and put their 12 months of desert warfare training into real fighting. At the fort's commissary, the Springfield Musketeers were having a beer and a coke and talking about the delays in going to war in Europe. Albert is starting to become ambivalent about being shipped overseas, "I know we are all eager for our battalion to be shipped to North Africa and to do our part in helping to end the war over there, but when we do go I'm really going to miss Judee. We have been dating for over six months now and she has told me that she really likes me. I have feelings for her too and my parents will be happy that I am dating a Chinese girl. My parents always told my siblings and me that we were suppose to choose a Chinese mate. The Chinese call White people "Bak Guwee" which means White Devils, and Colored people "Hauck Guwee" or Black Devils. I have yet to tell them about Judee because I'm going to break-up with her. When we finally get shipped to North Africa, she said that she would be waiting for me when I get back from Europe. I don't want her heart to be broken if I get killed in this war. It wouldn't be right for her to be waiting for someone who may not be coming back home." Tony tells Albert what he thinks, "I think you are nuts to think that way. Charlie and I think Judee is a wonderful gal and if she really likes you, she'll take a chance on love for a soldier going off to war." "Yes, but I'm not willing to take a chance on being serious about Judee when I don't even know how I will feel about her once this war is over which may go on for years. I just won't allow myself to get serious over Judee or anyone else not knowing what my future will be. There are going to be many military men who will not be coming back from this war, and it is best that there aren't a lot of loved ones waiting for them. To be honest, we haven't known each other that long and long-distance relationships aren't that successful. I think breaking up will also give Judee the freedom to meet new people without her feeling guilty about seeing others while I'm fighting overseas. I just don't want her to pin her hopes that I'll be coming back home to her, when so many unknown things can happen during this war. I hope you guys understand why I'm going to break-up with Judee tonight." Charlie interjects, "Breaking up with Judee now might be the best for her and for you as well. I know of four men in our company who have gotten letters from their girlfriends that absence did not make their hearts grow fonder, and that they were breaking up with them. Those guys are really upset and despondent that their girlfriends were not faithful to them now that they were in the Army. Tony comments, "Yeah, I remember the quote from John Greenleaf Whittier, "Of all sad words of tongue or pen, the saddest are these, 'It might have been."

****

Back at the joint Army-Navy headquarters, there was talk of blockading the Japanese in the Aleutians and letting them starve to death, but a blockade would be a long-term operation that would require many ships and men that were needed elsewhere. Also political pressure was being put on the military to remove the Japanese off Kiska and Attu Island. General Dewitt proposed to send a division of around 25,000 men to retake Kiska. The War Department decided to use the 7th Motorized Division under the command of General Brown to undertake the assignment. The rationalization was because the 7th Motorized Division was no longer needed in North Africa, and that they were stationed at Fort Ord, California. They were fit and in training for over a year, albeit for desert warfare, but they could be easily retrained in amphibious warfare on the California coast and be quickly loaded and shipped to Kiska. Most of the soldiers were draftees from California, Oregon, Washington, and from other western states. It was also referred to as the "California Division" because most of the soldiers were from California and included a regiment from the state's National Guard. The 7th Motorized Infantry Division had 14,235-men consisting of the 17th, 32nd, and the 159th infantry regiments. It had combat and combat support units, four artillery battalions, a combat engineer battalion, a medical battalion, a scout company, a reconnaissance company, a signal company, an ordnance company, a quartermaster company, a division headquarters company, a military police platoon and a counter-intelligence detachment.

The War Department put Admiral Kinkaid in overall command with Admiral Rockwell in charge as the amphibious force commander, General Brown as the ground commander, and Major General Butler, commander of the Eleventh Air Force, as air commander. A week later, the plan to take Kiska was put on hold in late January because President Roosevelt and Prime Minister Winston Churchill and their military staffs felt that the Kiska operation required too many men and ships that were needed in the "Europe First" strategy. The Joint Chiefs of Staff order the cancellation of the Kiska plan, but ordered the increase bombardment of Kiska instead. Admiral Kinkaid then put in a counter proposal to take Attu Island with a smaller force because intelligence estimated that only 500 Japanese were on Attu and that a 15,000-man infantry division would easily retake the island. Admiral King liked the plan and approved it on March 10, 1943. He also approved recommendations to build airbases on Attu Island and nearby Shemya Island for use against Japanese military installations in the Northern and Central Kuril Islands once the Japanese garrison on Attu Island was defeated. Unfortunately, the military planners had inaccurate U.S. Geological Survey maps that showed only terrain features 1000 yards from the shoreline. Additionally, they egregiously had no understanding of how the snow, fog, cold temperatures, constant cloud coverings, and high winds called the "williwaws" would inflict very serious injuries to their soldiers fighting on Attu Island.

Chapter 6
The Best Laid Plan has Gone Awry

In mid-March of 1943, the Springfield Musketeers were in their barrack packing up their gear in advance to being shipped to North Africa. Suddenly Captain Zenda rushes into the room and orders them to Headquarters Company. Tony asks, “What for Captain?” “Never mind. Just get your asses over there right now!” “Aye Aye Sir.” They hurried as fast as they could over the 200-yard field leading to headquarters and when there got there, they were ordered to the Special Operations room on the second floor. Two marines were standing guard at the doorway and saluted the three lieutenants as they cautiously entered the room scanning to see who was there. Seated at the head of a huge conference table, that seated 20, was Major Smith, along with other officers of the 2nd Battalion. Tony, Charlie, and Albert, although curious at seeing Major Smith, immediately saluted steadfastly. Major Smith acknowledged the three 2nd lieutenants, “At ease gentlemen. What you are going to learn today is highly classified and will determine if we are going to remove the Japanese from the Aleutians with the least amount of casualties. You might be asking yourselves how this involves you since the 17th Motorized Infantry Division has been training to go to North Africa. I'm sorry to inform you that the 17th will now be the 17th Light Infantry Division and sent to retake Attu Island from those godless Japanese. The decision was made by the War Department, and the 17th Infantry Regiment is to be the Assault Force, the 32nd in reserve and the 159th as the occupation force. As you can see the rest of the officers of the 17th are here, so please take a seat and I'll brief everyone as to why we have been chosen to do the dirty work.” Their hearts sank at learning that they will be going to Attu, but quietly took their seats. "As all of you know the Japanese have occupied Attu for almost eight months and have set-up a formidable strongholds. It became evident to the U.S. military that the Japanese were planning something big in the Aleutian Islands. Army Intelligence now estimates that there may be an elite regiment of around 2,000 soldiers under the commander of Colonel Yasuyo Yamasaki who earned the 'Order of the Rising Sun' which was awarded to him by the Emperor himself. He is one tough cookie and we better not underestimate his leadership. Intelligence and our code-breakers learned that the Japanese high command after the bombing of Pearl Harbor made plans to invade the islands of Kiska and Attu which are part of the Aleutian Chain and the territory of the United States of America. It should be noted that the Japanese are the first foreign power to invade and occupy the Continental United States since the War of 1812. They wanted those islands in order to control of the Western Pacific and Eastern Asia. They also wanted the islands as a diversion scheme to draw our Navy north to defend Attu and Kiska to conceal their strategic plan to attack and invade the island of Midway unopposed. As you know the plan did not work." Major Ealon Standeven, Executive Officer of the 2nd Battalion, interrupts, "Since we are a light infantry regiment now, we are going to need a lot of naval and air power to help dislodge those Japs who occupy the high ground. Some of those peaks are as high as 2,500 to 2,900 feet." "We will have plenty of air and naval support, but the mountains are usually covered with clouds, fog, and mist which will make it difficult to locate targets." Captain Paul Mackin asks, "When do you think the Department of War is planning to attack?" "It could be around May or June, so we'll have plenty of time to train for amphibious warfare at the Amphibious Corps of the Pacific Fleet which is in San Diego. It is under the command of U.S. Marine General Holland 'Howlin Mad' Smith who is an amphibious warfare expert. You will turn in your desert warfare gear and you will be issued cold weather and rain gear. I know this is a shocking turn of events and I hated it. The top brass at the War Department chose the 7th Army Division because we were the closest Army Division to the Aleutian Islands. Tomorrow meet at the airfield at 9:00 am. Okay, that's about it, meeting dismiss."

As Albert, Charlie, and Tony walk back to their barrack, Albert laments, "Damn, I just spent the last 12 months learning German, guess I should have learned Japanese." Tony says," Shit on us, why did we get picked to be the assault force. They usually end up with the highest casualty rate." Charlie mumbles, "I hate snow and cold weather." Now that the 7th Light Infantry Division was no longer the 7th Mechanized Infantry Division, they no longer had the use of armored personnel carriers, infantry fighting vehicles and M3 half-trucks to attack the enemy. Instead, they just had M1 rifles with M1 bayonets, M1 carbines, Browning automatic rifles (BAR), handguns, and cold weather clothes and boots to fight against the Japanese on Attu Island. Second lieutenants were issued Colt 1911A1 .45 automatic pistols. The next morning, the 17th Infantry was deployed to San Diego for an accelerated course in Pacific amphibious warfare because the timetable for "Operation Landgrab" to seize Attu Island was pushed ahead by a month. When the Springfield Musketeers arrived at the Army Amphibious Training Center, Tony rants, "They just put up this center last month, I hope they know what they are doing. Sunny San Diego beaches are not like Attu's permanently frozen ground under a layer of solid soil and the tundra consists of wet vegetation covered by soil." Albert tries to calm

Tony down, “Hey, let's just go with the flow of things and just learn how to get off landing barges without drowning.” Charlie remarks, “I hope they'll supply us with some really good rain and cold weather gear. I hear that frostbite is really nasty. Hey Albert, I read that the Chinese fear Frigophobia.” Albert looks at Charlie like he's nuts, “Huh, I never heard that.” “Yea, it has to do something with Yin and Yang. The Chinese fear being cold because it will sap their vitality and energy. They avoid cold things like the weather, cold drinks, and cold foods. When it is cold, they wear lots of warm clothes to keep their body temperature in balance.” “Well I don't believe in it, and anyway we went to College in Springfield, Massachusetts where the weather got as low as 18 degrees Fahrenheit in the winter. When I went skiing at the local ski resorts, I felt that my energy increased. So cold weather does not bother me.”

During their stay at the training center, the 17th Regiment learned the latest plans and hazards of amphibious landings. The officers were briefed on the plan for “Operation Landgrab,” by Major Smith. “Military reconnaissance has selected several ideal landing beaches on Attu Island, but they won't be chosen until we get there. The attack force will be split into two groups, Northern and Southern.” Captain Bjork of the 2nd battalion asks, “What Force will the 2nd battalion be in?” “The 2nd battalion will be in the Southern Force. The Japanese have fortified themselves in the upper mountains and ridges, so there should be minimal opposition to our beach landings. Intelligence also learned that Colonel Yamazaki doesn't have an elite regiment under his command, but second-rate troops consisting of older men and raw recruits from Hokkaido Island. However, they are led by seasoned officers and non-commissioned officers. General Brown predicts that we'll defeat them in three days. Are there any questions?" Major Standeven of the 2nd raises his hand, "I question the suitability of the clothing that is being issued to the men for Attu's cold weather climate. There are driving winds, mist, fog, and 40 degree temperatures on that island. The 17th Regiment has not been issued any cold weather gear, and will be wearing cloth clothing and jackets and carrying the same equipment that they trained with in the Mojave Desert." "General Brown believes that there are Japanese spies in San Francisco and wants them to think that we are shipping out to the tropical island of Midway, but winter gear will be below deck and issued later. Are there any more questions? If not, this briefing is over and you can go outside and see what companies the officers have been assigned to. Most of the companies remain intact, but some changes have been made because some companies were short 2nd lieutenants"

The company assignments:

E Company
Captain William F. Staab, CO
1st Lieutenant George E. Adams, XO-2nd in Command
2nd Lieutenant William A. Beeston, Platoon Leader
2nd Lieutenant William E. Copeland, Platoon Leader
2nd Lieutenant Raymond E. Bradbury, Platoon Leader
2nd Lieutenant William H. Beeston, Platoon Leader

F Company
Captain Delbert L Bjork, CO
2nd Lieutenant Albert P. Fong, XO-2nd in Command
2nd Lieutenant George W. Atwood, Platoon Leader
2nd Lieutenant Paul H. Brundage, Platoon Leader
2nd Lieutenant John Edrington, Platoon Leader
2nd Lieutenant Tony S. Ricci, Platoon Leader
2nd Lieutenant Harold W. Hahn, Platoon Leader

Company G
Captain Raymond E. Jones, CO
1st Lieutenant Robert L. Washnok, XO-2nd in Command
2nd Lieutenant Walter C. O'Niel, Platoon Leader
2nd Lieutenant Robert E. Little, Platoon Leader
2nd Lieutenant Francis J. Crohan, Platoon Leader
2nd Lieutenant Joseph S. Hunter, Platoon Leader

The posting of the company assignments were made on the last day of amphibious training in San Diego and lieutenants Fong, Ricci, and Atwood got on a military transport and flew back to Fort Ord, while the 17th Light Infantry Regiment was issued hot climate attire and embarked on transport ships in San Diego Harbor.

When Albert got back to the fort, he went straight to the commissary to call home to tell his parents that he was scheduled to go to Attu instead of Germany. “Hello dad? This is me” “Hi son, it is great to hear your voice again. Why are you calling?” “Dad, I got some bad news for you. The Army is sending me to Attu Island to fight the Japanese instead of going to Europe.” “I don't understand. Where is Attu Island?” “Attu is up around Alaska which is a territory of the United States.” “Are there a lot of Japanese soldiers up there?” “Well, there are about 2,000 of them, but we will have almost 15,000 army, navy, and air force men on our side. General Brown says that we should be able to defeat them in about three days.” “I'm not so sure it is going to be an easy fight. I read that they still think of themselves as Samurai warriors and they adhered to strict rules of combat, I think it is called 'Bushido.' In battle, they look forward to an honorable death. If they fail, they will commit ritual suicide called 'Seppuku.' They carry swords too and cut off their enemy's head!” “Only top officers do, and swords are no match for our bullets.”

"Well, you may be right, but still those Japanese soldiers are mean and cruel. The Chinese learned the hard way when they invaded China six years ago. Anyway I'll tell everyone the bad news." "The good news is that we are not going to ship out until late April, and I can come home for a week before we ship out. I'll tell you all the details when I get home. Okay, I got to hang-up now there are seven guys behind me that want to call their families. Love you. Bye!"

The next day, Albert, Charlie, and Tony were back in their barrack and Albert has a worried look on his face. "Hey guys, I know we don't want to talk about it and some will say it will bring bad luck, but I had a nightmare last night that one of us will be killed on Attu. I don't know who it was, I just saw a lot of dead U.S. Army soldiers on the soggy tundra covered in blood." Tony rolling his eyes says, "Man, I don't think you should think or talk that way. It's a bad omen." Charlie chiming in, "Yep, remember Julius Caesar and the Ides of March." "I know it was just a dream, but realistically the odds of being killed in major battles are quite high, and we are officers that lead from the front and not the back." Tony remembers a line from the Three Musketeers and boldly says, "Besides we are men, and after all it is our business to risk our lives." Charlie confidently reassures Albert, "And remember none of the Three Musketeers ever got killed in a fight." "Okay, I was wrong to mention my dream. Let's go and have lunch and than go to the firing range, I need some more practice firing uphill with gloves on."

It is now April 15th, 15 days before the 17th Light Infantry Regiment is scheduled to depart for Attu Island. Lieutenants Fong, Ricci, and Atwood get travel home leave for one week before they go to war. Albert calls home to tell mom that he is coming home. "Hello, this is Albee, is that you Alice?" "Of course this is your eldest sister. Have you forgotten my voice already little brother?" "Well, you are starting to sound like mother. How is everyone doing these days?" "I'm feeling well, why are you calling?" "I'm calling because I'm driving home today for a short stay before I have to go to Attu Island." "Oh my, I'll tell everyone that you are coming home today. Hurry up and get up here. And drive carefully." "Will do, I'll see you in about three hours, bye." When Albert arrived home the family gathered into the living room and he tells them about his Pacific amphibious training in San Diego and when he'll be shipping off to Attu Island. "I'll be shipping out at the end of this month to Attu Island. My regiment along with air force and naval support will land on Attu Island to attack the Japanese. There is only about 2,000 Japanese on the island, but they are not suppose to be an elite unit. However, we will have close to 15,000 soldiers, so we should easily defeat them." Father Fong cautions his son, "I agree that you will have the numbers advantage, but remember random bad luck can get even the strongest soldier killed." Albert reassures his father, "My combat training skills along with the 'Fit and Ferocious' men of my company F, gives me the confidence that I will come back alive. Maybe wounded, but not in a flag draped coffin." Father replies, "I'm really afraid for you and your men who are going to Attu to fight those crazy Japanese soldiers who worship their Emperor Hirohito. Remember what the Japanese did in 1937 to the Chinese at Nanking during the Sino-Japanese War? They butchered nearly 150,000 prisoners of war, 50,000 male civilians, and raped close to 20,000 women and girls. I think that Roosevelt was so afraid that anyone of Japanese ancestry living on the West Coast of this country, even those who are American citizens, may still be loyal to Emperor Hirohito. This was probably the reason that he issued Executive Order 9066 that sent anyone with a Japanese last name or heritage to ten relocation camps in seven states." Albert nods disapproval, "Fear causes people, even Presidents, to do stupid and illogical things." Mother Fong speaks up saying, "The poor Hashimoto family down the street were sent to the relocation camp in Poston, Arizona, and Betty and Kenji Tanaka were sent to Tule Lake War Relocation Center, California."

Albert then thinks about Leslie's wife Dorothy, who is half of the famous dance team of "Toy and Wing." They are billed as the Chinese "Ginger Rogers and Fred Astaire," but she is really Japanese, Dorothy Takahashi. He asks Leslie, "Will Dorothy have to go to one of those relocation camps?" Leslie shakes his head, "No, she is dancing in New York and will stay there until this war is over. She and her dance partner Paul Wing, were scheduled to do a movie with some big-name Hollywood movies stars, but it was canceled because the studio found out that Dorothy was Japanese. Also Paul got drafted and assigned to the 304th Tank Brigade commanded by General Patton." Mother Fong calls the family for lunch, "Everyone come into the kitchen. I made beef chow fun and chicken chow mein for lunch."

****

When Tony got home he was glad to see his father William, even his stepmother Irene. "Hi dad, I'm glad that the army gave me a leave to see you before I ship out to Attu. I'm sure it's because some of the guys won't be coming home after the war." "Irene, come quick, Tony just got in!" Irene comes out of kitchen, "Hello Tony, it is so good to see you before you ship out. I understand that you are going to some island in Alaska to fight the

Japanese." "That is correct Irene, but I rather fight the Nazis in Europe." "Well, I hate those Nazis too! You know that I am Jewish, my maiden name is Irene Kofman. I loathe the Germans and what they are doing to the Jews" "So what are they doing to the Jews that is so bad?" "I heard from my aunt Fanny Rosenberg who lives in Poland that the Nazis just built a concentration camp at Auschwitz and are sending Jews there to be exterminated." "I heard rumors to that effect too, but I don't think it is true." "Irene lives in Warsaw and many Pols claim to have seen train cars filled with Jews going to Auschwitz." "Well the Nazis may be sending them to work camps, but they are not going to execute them." "Even sending them to work camps are a crime. I hope our American soldiers will kill as many as they can!" William butts in, "Okay Irene, cool down or you're going to have a heart-attack. Shouldn't you go back to the kitchen and start making dinner? I'm going to take Tony on a ride in our new 1940 Ford Deluxe." "You bought a Deluxe?" "Sure did! Let's go for a ride." Tony and his father go out the front door, and Irene goes back into the kitchen.

****

When Charlie arrived home in Chicago, he rang the door bell and his mother Janet answered the door. "Hi mom, I just got in." "Hello Charlie, give your mom a big kiss." "Les, Charlie just arrived." "I'm coming. Charlie, it's so good that you are home, but sad to know that you are shipping out to some place called Attu Island to fight the Japanese. I thought that the Germans were going to be hard to defeat, but now I think the Japs are going to be harder than the Krauts." "I think so too because Hitler made a big mistake going into Russia." "I know. I've been reading about the Germans invading Russia in the

Daily Herald." "Yes, Army intelligence says that the German code-name for their invasion is 'Operation Barbarossa.' They estimate that the invading German Army consists of 150 divisions which is close to three million soldiers, 3,000 tanks, and 7,000 artillery pieces. The Russians are formidable too and they will turn back the German Army especially if the fighting lags on into winter. Remember Napoleon made that same mistake." Charlie turns to his mother Janet, "Mom, how are you feeling? Have the doctors come up with any new ways to cure cancer?" "Yes, they just started to use radiation machines to try to kill cancer cells. Its called radiation therapy. The doctors hope it will kill the cancer cells or at least slow their growth." "Your mother and I are praying to God that this radiation machine will kill those cells and that she and I will be able to grow old together to see many grandchildren." "I hope that machine will work because Mary Jo and I plan on having two children after we get married when I get out of the army. A girl for her and a boy for me. We're going out for dinner tonight and she wants you two join us. Okay?" "We'd love to." "And after dinner, we'll all go over to the 'Trianon Ballroom' to dance the night away. I've never been there, but Mary Jo says it's the world's most beautiful ballroom. She says it was inspired by the Grand Trianon Palace at Versailles." Janet adoringly says, "Charlie, you're the best son in the world." "That's because you're the best mom in the world."

****

The week of leave was way too short as Tony, Charlie, and Albert kissed their families goodbye while pondering if it could be the last time they would see them. After they got back to Fort Ord, they had to attend many strategy meetings with top-brass and training sessions with the men of Company F as they prepared for their departure to do battle with the Japanese.

As the days moved closer to the planned attack on Attu Island, Major Smith scheduled a briefing on the final plans of “Operation Landgrab” with all the officers of the 17th Infantry Regiment. “Gentlemen today you will learn the final details of our mission to take back the Island of Attu and we will kill and remove everyone of those Japanese devils for what they did to us at Pearl Harbor.” All the officers cheer and yell wildly. “Our Attu assault force D-Day will be May 4th. Intelligence suddenly projected that the Japanese now have 2,400 soldiers, but we still out-number them 6 to 1, and we should be able to take Attu back in less than a week. For the last 60 days, our Army Air Force, along with elements of the Royal Canadian Air Force have been bombing and strafing Japanese positions and facilities on Kiska and Attu. In addition to the aerial attacks, the Heavy Cruiser USS Salt Lake City has been bombarding the Japs. Now that the Army Air Force and the Navy have soften them up, it is now the Army's turn to deliver the Coup de Grâce. We will fly to San Francisco in three days to embark on vessels and join our regiments which are on their way to Attu Island. That is all for now except for 2nd lieutenants Washnok, Elliot, Fong, Mcgee, and Adams.” Elliot speaks for the group, “Yes, Major Smith, you wanted to see us?” “Yes gentlemen, all of your commanding officers have recommend you for promotions to 1st lieutenants for your exemplary duty and leadership skills, and as such, I have approved them. So thank your captains and go and exchange your gold bars for silver bars.” Each lieutenant thanks Major Smith and salutes him as they exit the room with euphoric smiles on their faces.

After picking up his silver bars, 1st Lieutenant Fong goes back to his barrack to tell Tony and Charlie about his promotion. “Look what I got guys, I just got promoted to 1st lieutenant. I thought that Captain Bjork was going to choose lieutenant Reynolds who was a West Point graduate.” Charlie and Tony shake Albert's hand. Tony congratulates his very good friend, “Congratulations Albert. You will make a great XO, the men really like and respect you.” Charlie touched the silver bars on Albert's epaulettes, congratulates him, and says, “These bars are made out of real silver. The 2nd lieutenant's bars are called gold, but they are made out of brass. We need to Brasso them to keep them shiny. Let's go over to the commissary and celebrate your promotion. Tony and I will get our favorite Hamm's beer and we will get you your favorite non-alcoholic Coca Cola.” “I'll meet you guys at the commissary because I want to run over and thank Captain Bjork for my promotion.” Albert goes over the headquarters of F Company and walks into Bjork's office, “Captain Bjock, I hope I'm not interrupting you, but I want to thank you for recommending me for promotion to Major Smith. I didn't think you would choose me when Reynolds and Hahn are West Point grads.” “Well let me tell you Fong, your personnel record indicated that your Springfield College grades were higher than Hahn's and Reynolds' West Point grades, but more importantly your command communication and combat tactical skills are better than theirs. That is why I chose you.” “Well thank you again sir. I assure that when we fight those Japanese on Attu, I promise I won't let you down. I'm true to our 7th Infantry Division's motto: Trust in Me.” “1st lieutenant Fong, I know I made the right choice. Now get out of here. I've got a ton of paperwork to do.”

Fong goes over to the Commissary and finds Tony,

Charlie, and Sergeant Hector Manly of F Company, “Hey Charlie, Tony, and Sergeant Manly.” “Lieutenant Fong, I see you were promoted to 1st lieutenant. Congratulations and now you will be the executive officer of our company.” “That is correct and I'm making you the BAR man in your squad. They call the BAR M1918A2 a light machine gun, but it weighs almost 25 pounds fully loaded with a bipod. It's 47 inches long, bulky, and difficult to carry in battle. It needs a big man to carry it and you are one of the biggest and strongest men in our company.” “Lieutenant Fong, I'll be proud to be a BAR man.” “Sergeant Manly, how are the men feeling about being the Army's first major amphibious operation?” “To tell you the truth, many of them are scared, and many are upset that they trained for desert warfare, and now they have to fight in snow, fog, freezing temperatures, and muddy tundra. Some of the men fear the fog, cold and snow more than the Japs. They believe that we will not be given sufficient time to acclimate to the harsh weather of Attu Island. They also don't think their leather boots will stay dry after a day or two.” “I agree and I will see if I can get Major Smith to get some rain proof boots for our men,” Albert turns to Charlie and Tony who are each drinking a can of Hamm's beer, and in a kidding manner says, “Hey guys, where the heck is my bottle of Coca Cola.”

Chapter 7
Operation Landgrab Begins

Three days later, the 17th Light Infantry Regiment gather at Fort Mason in San Francisco in preparation for their assault on Attu Island. Lieutenant Fong meets with Captain Bjork, "My family lives in Vallejo and my dad owns a twelve unit apartment building in San Francisco and ten of the units are rented to our relatives." "I was here on vacation with my wife about five years ago, and we really loved the city. After the war ends, we'll be coming back to the States by way of San Francisco and hopefully you can give me a tour of the city." "I would love to do that." "I hope General Brown's prediction that this battle will be over in three days is accurate, but he's been known to be an optimist. On the other hand, General Ruckner told me that Attu is going to be tough and that our infantry is going to have to go in there with corkscrews to dig out the Japs." "Captain, you better order some corkscrews for our men." Both officers laugh and head off to the transport ships.

On April 24th, the 17th sailed out of San Francisco Bay under the Golden Gate Bridge into the Pacific escorted by Naval Forces to support the landings at Attu Island. It consisted of the Battleships Pennsylvania, Idaho, Nevada, the Escort Carrier Nassau for close air support, and 29 other vessels. The Navy also sent 2 heavy cruisers, 6 light cruisers, and 8 destroyers to the west of Attu to defend the island against the Japanese Navy if they try to send ground troops to rescue their garrison on the island of Attu.

On April 30th, the attack force arrived at Cold Bay on the Alaska peninsula, but 3-star Admiral Kinkaid who was in command of "Operation Landgrab" was not there because he was on Adak Island. The generals on the attack transport Zelin had a meeting to make sure each of them knew their part and responsibility in "Operation Landgrab." The generals at the meeting were, 2-star Generals Albert Brown, John DeWitt, Eugene Landrum, and Archibald Arnold. It was General Dewitt who believed that right after the bombing of Pearl Harbor, that Japanese nationals and Japanese Americans in the West Coast of the United States were conspiring to sabotage the American war effort. He went to President Roosevelt and convinced him to issue Executive Order 9066 giving the military authority, under his command, to incarcerate some 110,000 Japanese men, women and children, most of whom were American citizens to relocation camps.

General Brown looking over plaster mockups of the battle area, opens the meeting by saying, "Based on weather conditions, Admiral Kinkaid has chosen Plan E. D-Day Attu will be May 7th and 0600 hours will be H-Hour. As you know the most favorable landing beaches are Yellow and Blue Beaches in Massacre Bay. The Attack Force will be split into two groups, Northern and Southern. The 2nd Battalion, 17th Infantry less company H will be the first wave and land at Blue Beach on the right side of Massacre Bay. The 3rd Battalion will be the second wave and land at Yellow Beach, with half of the units on the right and the other half on the left side of Massacre Bay. Lieutenant Colonel Hartl will direct the landing at Red Beach in Holtz Bay to support the remainder of the landings. The Japanese have fortified their mountain strongholds, but our battleship guns and Army Air Force B-24 and B-25 bombers will hammer those fortifications so it will be easy for our infantry to annihilate Yamasaki's garrison. I don't think it is going to take longer then three days to defeat the Japanese."

It was on May 4th, after the final plan and preparations were passed down the chain of command, that the assault force sailed out of Cold Bay into the windy and freezing waters of the North Pacific passing the Aleutians and into the Bering Sea. The convoy was led by the battleships and destroyer escorts in search of any Japanese naval ships near Attu Island.

Meanwhile the Japanese prepare for battle.

On the morning of May 4th, at the headquarters of the 2nd Sector, North Sea Garrison, Colonel Yasuyo Yamasaki is meeting with his top officers to issue his final orders on the defense of Attu against the overwhelming forces of the American Army. At the meeting are Captains Hiroyuki Numata and Jiro Tsuya of the 2nd Sector, Lieutenant Colonel Hiroshi Yonekawa of the North Kuril Fortress, Major Tokuji Watanabe of the 303rd Infantry Battalion, Captain Chinzo Ono of the 302nd Engineer Company, and Captain Toshio Hobokabe of the Artillery Battalion. Colonel Yamasaki addresses his officers, "I have very bad news. I just received word from Naval Headquarters that the three supply ships have been either sunk or turned back to Japan by the U.S. Navy blockade. We are already short of ammunition and food. Vice Admiral Hosogaya of the Fifth Fleet assured me that if we could hold off the Americans for two weeks, it would give enough time for the Navy to send a naval task force to get here and rescue us. So implement 'hit and run' tactics which will prolong this coming battle and give time for the naval task force to get here." Yamasaki asks Major Watanabe, "When do you think the Americans are going to attack?" "Based on our intelligence, the Americans are at Cold Water Bay. I would guess they will come in about 4 or 5 days depending on the weather." "How many Nambu machine guns nests does the 303 Infantry have on the ridges above Massacre and

Holtz Bays?" "We have 20 set up overlooking Massacre and 15 set up overlooking Holtz. We also moved the two 75-millimeter mountain guns atop the ridge which can cover both arms of Holtz Bay. Those 'stupid round eyes' will be easy targets when they advance up the mountains and ridges" "Hobokabe did you move the 70-millimeter light howitzers to the Holtz Bay emplacements and the anti-aircraft guns to Massacre Bay?" "Yes Colonel. I also placed Type 88 dual purpose guns 100 yards on both sides of the howitzer and the gun crews can now fire 20 rounds a minute." "Excellent! Captain Tsuya, did you finally complete the camouflaging of the barracks and supply building on the West Arm of Holtz Bay?" "Yes colonel, you couldn't tell if there were buildings there from the air or on the ground 100 feet away." "Great, I was worried that it could be easily bombed from the air. Captain Numata, did you double up the number of grenade launchers and throwers surrounding Massacre Bay?" "Yes sir, and our three man launcher crew can fire up to 25 rounds a minute. Those 'American Joes' will be retreating down the mountains faster than scared rabbits." "Maybe so, but don't underestimate those 'Joes,' I heard that over in Europe they are winning a lot of battles against the Nazis. Okay, now let's get ready for 'Great War,' everyone get back to your units and put the men on Red Alert and tell them not to waste their ammunition because our supply ships have been turned back by the American Navy."

The Americans arrive at Attu Island.

On May 7th, the Attu assault force arrived at Massacre and Holtz Bays ready to invade Attu. The generals and admirals gathered together to confirm if D-Day is a go, but General Brown received a message from Admiral

Kinkaid to postpone D-Day due to high winds and corresponding surf on the landing beaches. General Brown tells the generals to pass down the word that D-Day will be delayed until calm weather permits a landing. The weather forecasters predict that these unfavorable conditions will last for a couple more days. On the 10th of May, the weather improved and General Brown received word from Admiral Kinkaid, “General Brown, good news, the weather forecasters are predicting clear weather tomorrow” “Well, that is what I have been waiting for.” “D-Day will go forward as planned, only four days late. Pass the word down to all the commanding generals and officers that we are disembarking onto Attu Island tomorrow.”

Word is passed down to all the men of the 17th Regiment that tomorrow will be D-Day and that H-hour will be 0700 hours. Captain Bjork passes the word along to his men of F Company, 2nd Battalion, “Listen up men, tomorrow is the day we've been waiting for. We all know that it is not going to be a walk in the park. The Japs have been on Attu for over six month and dug in on the high ground 1000 to 2400 feet high. The terrain in the low areas consists of spongy muskeg, soggy unfrozen soil, making vehicular travel, even tracked vehicles difficult if not impossible. I know that some of you may feel scared, but we all feel scared and if anyone says that they are not, they're lying. I want everyone to keep your wits about you even if bullets are flying around you. I won't order you to do anything that I wouldn't do myself. I have assigned Lieutenant Fong to command Platoon A, Lieutenant Atwood to command Platoon B, Lieutenant Brundage to command to Platoon C, Lieutenant Reynolds to command Platoon D, Lieutenant Ricci to command Platoon E, and Lieutenant Hahn to Platoon F.

When we hit the sands of Blue Beach, I want you to

remember what Company F stands for." The men shout in unison, "First, Fit, and Fearsome!" "You all will be issued field packs with a day's worth of K rations, water purification tablets, a canteen of water, a mess kit, a change of socks and underwear, a sleeping bag, and shelter halves. I want you to grease your boots to water proof them. And don't forget to sharpen your bayonets. Okay, that is it for now, Get prepared for tomorrow, get a good night's sleep because wake-up call will at 0500 hours."

Lieutenants Fong, Ricci, and Atwood get together to talk about the forthcoming battle. Charlie voices his concerns, "I think greasing our leather boots are not going to keep our feet dry for more than a couple of days." Fong agrees, "They should have given us a pair of rubber fishing boots to slip over our leather boots." Tony isn't worried, "I think we'll be okay as long as it doesn't rain too much. I'm more worried about the Japs controlling the high sharp and narrow ridges that will make it difficult to spot them, let alone get close to them to use our bayonets. You can't shoot what you can't see." Fong ponders, "I don't understand why the 11th Army Air Force hasn't carpet bombed the Japanese to Hell with their B-25 bombers." "Charlie answers, "It's probably because those mountains and ridges are usually covered in clouds, fog, and mist." Tony agrees, "Yep, there aren't many clear skies over Attu that's for sure. I know once the fighting starts, we'll be spread out in separate platoons climbing up those damn mountains, but remember guys, we're still, all for one and one for all." Tony, Charlie and Albert bump fists and say, "Always and forever."

Chapter 8
D-Day Attu Island

On May 11, 1943, the battleship Nevada, six destroyers and seven other ships got into positions to support the Southern Force landings at Massacre Bay. The battleships Pennsylvania and Idaho along with six destroyers got into position at Holtz Bay to support the Northern Force landings. The attack transports, Harris, Heywood, and Zeilin carrying the Southern Force and the J. Franklin Bell carrying the Northern Force arrived in the transport area at 0719 hours and anchored. Word came down at 0840 hours to "lower all boats" for the first assault wave, but the fog caused the boats to circle for six hours until the fog cleared. By 1500 hours all the boats landed unopposed by the Japanese.

Major Smith leading his men of the 2nd Battalion, 17th Infantry Regiment landed on Blue Beach on the right side of the Massacre Bay and sets up his headquarters 100 yards from the shoreline. Captain Bjork leads the 300-man Company F up Massacre Valley along the right flank of the Southern Force. Captain Bjork gives lieutenant Fong his first orders, "Fong take A and B platoons over to secure the mountain pass between Massacre Valley and Sarana Valley. Platoons C, D, E, and F follow me to the left." As Fong and Atwood lead their platoons, Fong says, "Charlie, it doesn't seem right that there was no gun fire from the Japs when we landed." "I know, I think the Japs are waiting until we start advancing up these muddy and snow covered ridges. Right now we can't see the top of the ridges, but I bet they can see us. Damn, there aren't any trees or large boulders to hide behind when they start shooting. We are unprotected targets." "Tell the men to fan out in squads, I don't want them grouped together when the Japs start firing at us." As they cautiously move through the slush and mud towards Sarana Valley, they encounter sporadic fire from the ridges above them. The men take cover and return fire up the ridges. “Sergeant Manly, take your squad around those boulders and see if you can take out those Japs on our right.” “My pleasure sir.” Manly and his squad quickly locate four Japanese soldiers, but they shoot and kill two and wound one of Manly's squad before he fires his Browning Automatic Rifle killing all of them. The Japanese Arisaka bolt-action rifles are no match against a BAR that can fire 650 rounds per minute, but the magazine only holds 20 rounds. Manly, who carries 15 extra magazines, shouts at Private Tilly to get the medics to take care of the three fallen casualties. After platoon A secures the pass between the two valleys, Lieutenant Fong sees that Lieutenant Atwood's platoon B is coming under heavy fire from a platoon of Japanese soldiers on the ridge between Alexai Pass and Massacre Valley. He orders half of his platoon of 47 men to remain and protect the pass between Massacre and Sarana Valleys leaving Sergeant Manly in charge. He then takes the other half of his platoon and rushes over to help platoon B. When Lieutenant Fong and his men join in the fire fight, Fong sees a Japanese soldier with his rifle and bayonet rushing towards him. He fires his Colt .45 pistol hitting him with a head shot and moves on to shoot and kill another Japanese soldier. The fight continues on for another five minutes and the Americans were able to kill 19 Japanese soldiers before the remaining soldiers retreated into the upper mountains. Once the firing was over, Fong realized that 5 of his men were killed, 5 were seriously wounded, and 3 with minor wounds. Lieutenant Atwood was unhurt, but he counted 4 of his men killed, 6 seriously wounded, and 5 with minor wounds. Charlie is happy to see Albert, “Good show buddy, we were ambushed by those Japs and my first sergeant was shot in the head before we knew that they were there." "It looks like we've taken about 10 casualties and this is just our first day on this cursed island." "Let's call the medics to carry our dead and wounded down to the base hospital. Private Williams, get some medics up here quickly before some of our men bleed to death. Hurry up!" "Yes sir." "Charlie, I have to get back to my platoon. Hope to see you back at camp, and watch out for those sneaky snipers." "Will do, and you too."

As the battalions struggled to make little progress up the mountains, the 48th Field Artillery set up two 105-millimeter howitzers M3 batteries on wooden platforms on solid ground. Then forward observers were sent with the infantry to radio back distances, directions, and gun elevations to Japanese positions.

Captain Bjorks leads his platoons to the foot of a ridge leading to a creek due east of Massacre Bay. He wants to provide left flank security for platoons A and B if they can reach the top of the ridge, but the map that he has does reflect the harshness of a ravine that will make their assent to the top of the ridge difficult and slow.

Suddenly the platoons come under intense fire from a platoon from the 665-man 303rd Independent Infantry Battalion under the command of Major Tokuji Watanabe. The Japanese not only had terrain advantage, they also had two Type 99 Nambu light machine gun nests and a 37-millimeter anti-tank gun. Captain Bjork orders his men to halt, "Men, take cover and sink into your positions and fire at will." With deadly bullets and hand grenades flying in both directions, many soldiers of the 303rd and the men of Company F were killed and wounded. With American casualties growing after fighting for 15 minutes, Captain Bjork realizes that they are in a losing position. “Men, I'm ordering a retreat, so get your asses back down to the foot of this ravine.” When the men struggled back down the mountain, carrying their dead and wounded comrades to safety, Lieutenants Brundage, Reynolds, Hahn, and Ricci count the number of dead and wounded. They report the count to Captain Bjork, “Jesus Christ, we've lost 11 men and 16 are injured and half of them need to go to the hospital. Men, we're done for the day and heading back to our base camp to regroup, rest, and reorganize our platoons. Then we'll go back tomorrow to even the score with those Japs of the 303rd.”

****

The 3rd Battalion, 17th Infantry under the command of Major James Montague, landed on the left side of Yellow Bay and received scattered rifle fire. As they advanced further up the rugged mountainsides, they encountered increased rifle, machine gun fire, and light artillery fire from three Type 41 75-millimeter light howitzers from the shelf in front of Massacre-Holtz Bay Pass. The Japanese soldiers were from the 420-man Northern Kuril Fortress Infantry commanded by lieutenant Colonel Hiroshi Yonekawa.

Major Montague halts his men, “Captain Foulston order the men to build a defensive position and fire at will. Call up the forward observation team to locate those mountain guns.” “Sergeant Barns, have the FO team send the coordinates of those mountain guns that are pinning us down and killing our men.” A soldier next to Barnes gets shot through his left cheek, splattering blood all over Sergeant Barnes, as he falls dead into the mud. The Americans return fire from their M1s and Browning Automatic Rifles, but they are no match for the heavy guns and grenades exploding all around them. They can't use their grenades because Japanese are over 75 yards on the mountain above them. The 3rd Battalion is suffering heavy casualties and need to destroy those howitzers or they will have to retreat.

Finally the forward observation team reached a spot where it could locate the three Japanese mountain guns and machine gun nest over-looking the 3rd Battalion. They immediately radioed the coordinates of those guns to the fire direction center next to the 105-millimeter howitzers and its 10-man crews, and two rounds screamed up the valley. The observers recorded the explosions and called in the corrections. Other rounds were fired until the right coordinates bracketed those mountain guns. Then the observers gave the order to "fire for effect," and the M3 howitzers fired 20 of its 39-pound shells on the Japanese. It totally demolished the machine gun nest and those 75-millimeter howitzers with their 3-man crews. Now unimpeded, Major Montague tells Captain Foulston, "Call for the medics to take care of the dead and wounded. The rest of the Japs are retreating up to towards the mountains, so lets check the men who are wounded to see how many of them can still fire their weapon and make it up to Massacre-Holtz Bay Pass. Tell the forward advance team that they did a great job."

When the casualty report is given to Major Montague, he shakes his head in anger. "Those damned guns did a number on us. 21 dead, 26 seriously wounded, and 16 with minor wounds." Now unimpeded, Major Montague gives the orders to move cautiously up the mountains, "Major Wallace order the men to advance up to the pass at the head of Massacre Bay and once we secure it, our next objective is to secure the Massacre-Sarana Pass area." "Will do Jim."

Meanwhile, Colonel Edward Earle, Commander of 17th Infantry Regiment and of the Southern Assault Force landed at Massacre Bay with 2,000 men. At Holtz Bay, Colonel Frank Curlin commander of the 1st Battalion, 17th Infantry Regiment and of the Northern Assault Force landed at Red Beach with 1,600 men. Both battalions landed on the Beaches unopposed.

Although the troops landed unopposed, The battleships Idaho and Pennsylvania bombarded the Japanese in Chichagof Harbor by radar for an hour in the morning. In the afternoon, they bombarded the Japanese in Holtz Bay area attempting to destroy their 75-millimeter gun positions. Also adding to the bombardment was the destroyer Phelps.

Four fighters were launched from the deck of the Nassau dropping propaganda leaflets over Chichagof Harbor alerting the Japanese that the invasion was underway. On the fighters return to the escort carrier, two pilots were unable to locate it due to the fog and ditched there planes in the icy waters near the destroyer Aylwin and were rescued. The two other planes crashed upon landing. The deck crews pushed them over the side. This was the first close air support mission flown from an aircraft carrier in support of ground troops. Tragically four fighters were lost just to drop leaflets to the Japanese that the Americans were coming. Needless to say, the Japanese were well aware that the Americans were coming.

At 2100 hours, General Brown and his staff came ashore and set up their command post near Lake Elwood. This was the start of a very long battle that would not be over in 3 days.

Chapter 9
Snow, Fog, Wind, and Cold are Bitter Enemies

The weather on D-Day when the 17th Infantry Regiment stormed the beaches of Attu, it was foggy, cloudy, wet and cold. It hindered artillery and naval gun fire and disrupted radio communications as well. The temperature was in the low 40 degrees Fahrenheit. It was forecasted that precipitation, wind, rain, snow, and mist would persist for the whole month of May. After the second day of the invasion of Attu by the 17th and 32nd Light Infantry Regiments, the men started to suffer the ills caused by the weather. The wind-driven cold rain soon saturated their clothes and field jackets causing hypothermia. The rain and water in the terrains seeped into their leather boots causing trench foot which kills tissue and produces excruciating pain.

By Saturday May 15, 1943, only four days after D-Day Attu, most of the American forces were bogged down by the Japanese and the inhospitable weather on Attu Island. Company F, 2nd Battalion, 17th Infantry are camped on a mountain overlooking Holtz Bay. At 1800 hours, Captain Bjork calls his lieutenants for a briefing. “Men, tomorrow when hopefully this fog and mist dissipates, we're going to attack a platoon size force from the 303rd Independent Infantry Battalion on the other side of this hill. They're waiting for us, so they know we're coming. If the fog doesn't lift or if we get heavy winds and rain, it will be a 'no go.' Hell, this damned fog is so thick I can't see more than 25 feet through it. How are your men doing and what are your platoon count? Lieutenant Fong answers, “My platoon is down to 37 men and they are freezing because their field jackets, pants, and boots are really damp and wet. Eight were killed, four were wounded, but Private Nelson looked like he won't make it, and two had to go to the hospital for trench foot" Lieutenant Ricci speaks next, "My platoon now has 40 men and all of them are cold and wet. Three of them are really sick and can't see straight to fire their rifles. Four were killed and three were wounded." Lieutenant Brundage answers, "I'm down to 40 men, 5 were killed, five were seriously wounded and four of my men had to help carry the dead bodies of private Wilson and private Olson back to the morgue at the base camp because we couldn't get any medics to carry them away." Lieutenant Atwood says, "I'm sad to report sir, that I loss a fifth of my platoon. Five were killed, five wounded, and three had trench foot, so I sent them to the base hospital. My platoon B count is 37." The next to report was Lieutenant Reynolds, "Platoon D's strength is 38 men, Captain. Five have been killed, two wounded and six have weather related injures. The medics took all of them to the hospital. My platoon has suffered more casualties from the weather than from the Japs." Lieutenant Hahn reports, "My men are down to 42."

Captain Bjork empathizes with the lieutenants for the loss of their men and thanks them for their courageous leadership. "This battle is not going as planned. The top brass didn't issue us the proper wear for this cold weather climate. Hell, the Japs that we've killed have warmer clothing than we do. Their boots are water-proof too." Lieutenant Ricci interjects,"Two of my men with small feet took some dead Japs boots to wear because they said they kept their feet dry. Albert and Charlie, you should pass the word down to your platoons that swapping out dead Jap's boots for our water soaked ones isn't a bad idea." Charlie objects, "I'm not going to wear some stinking Jap's boots!" "Well, it's better than having your feet turn red or bluish in color, swell and smell of decay. If it gets really bad, it can kill the tissues in the foot and cause a lot of pain. The doctors might even have to amputate the foot. And I'll take a dead Jap's boots if I feel I'm coming down with trench foot, but I don't think any of those Japs wear a shoe size 13." Albert ponders, "I wish we could build a fire to at least dry out our socks, but it would give away our position and that would be stupid."

Captain Bjork stops the discussion about taking dead Japanese boots, and explains the plan of attack once the fog lifts. "Okay, enough about dead Japs' boots. Now that I know the numbers and strength of our men, I've decided to make a few changes. As we know, the Japanese are waiting for us on the other side of the hill. I checked out their defense and they are using the 'Reverse Slope' defense that Wellington used against Napoleon at Waterloo. So, instead of using the full force of our company to meet them head on, Fong and I will lead platoons A, C, D and F up to the top of the hill, faking an attack on the center of their defense, but stop at the crest before we hit the reverse slope which will openly expose us the to their fire. Instead, lieutenant Ricci's platoon will circle around the Japs left flank and Lieutenant Atwood's platoon will circle around their right flank and attack. When I see their forces moving to defend their flanks, weakening their center, I'll come over the hill and attack the center. Atwood and Ricci, when you attack don't get nearer to them than 75 yards and out of hand grenade range until we come over the hill and attack the center." "Okay lieutenants, head back to your platoons and get ready to move out tomorrow. I got to write up my daily report and send it over to General Brown down at Headquarters."

On the morning of the 16th of May, the fog surrounding the lower mountains of Attu Island lifts that allows Captain Bjork to execute his plan to attack the

Japanese on the other side of the hill at 0900 hours. "Lieutenants Ricci and Atwood lead your platoons and set up on their flanks keeping out of rifle range and waited there until I radio you the give word to open fire on them. We'll be waiting below the crest of the hill where the Japs can't see us. They will think that we are attacking them with a Pincer Movement and turn their fire and attention on their flanks. Once I see that, I'll come over the hill and attack their center. You guys are going to take a beating until we get there, so don't be any heroes and don't come in with bayonets on until we attack their center. Radio us when the both of you get into position." Lieutenant Atwood says, "Ricci and I think it will take us about 30 minutes to get into position if all goes will." "Okay, get on your way now."

When platoons B and E set up on the flanks of the Japanese, Captain Bjork radios them to attack the Japanese company of around 230 soldiers. When the firefight intensifies between the two American platoons and the Japanese, Captain Bjork and 1st lieutenant Fong who is the executive officer, lead platoons A, C, D and F totaling 159 men over the hill and charge fearlessly down and into the center of the Japanese's defense. Platoons B and E enter the fight from the flanks with bayonets blazing. Within 20 minutes of fighting, the Japanese who were totally confused and surrounded on three sides are quickly defeated and killed. Not one Japanese soldier was willing to surrender because the Americans soon learned that the Japs lived by the code of "Bushido" which to the Japanese warrior value death and honor above life and surrender. Although Captain Bjork's Company F, won their firefight with the Japanese, the victory came a high price. Lieutenant Fong brings the bad news to Captain Bjork, "Captain, we took a terrible beating today, 25 men were killed including Lieutenant

Brundage, 20 seriously wounded including Sergeant Ford, and 11 lightly wounded. Lieutenant Ricci says that his ears are ringing from a grenade blast." "How did Brundage die?" "He got hit the chest by three bullets, probably was killed instantly. Reynolds got lucky when a bullet glanced off his helmet and he is okay. The medics are taking the dead and the badly wounded men to the hospital. Our company is now down to 189 men. Poor Brundage, he was one of the nicest guys I every met. He said that he was going to marry his sweetheart Jane after he got out of the Army. So many of our guys that got killed were so young. I think Privates Wiggins, Cooper, and Owens were under 20 and corporal Larsen told me just before D-Day that he turned 25." "Fong, I know how you feel and it only makes me hate the Japs even more. Go and check on the morale of our men and report back to me." "Will do captain."

Company F didn't have much time to rest and enjoy their victory because Captain Bjork received orders to support Company B of the 2nd Battalion, 32nd Infantry in their battle to defend Massacre-Holtz Bay Pass. "Okay men, we are needed to help the 2nd B, 32nd I over at Massacre-Holtz Bay Pass. The medics are coming to take care of the dead and wounded. The rest of you pack up your gear and get ready to beat the hell out of some more Japs. Hurry up, we move out in 15 minutes."

****

Back at the 7th Infantry Division headquarters, General Brown sent three messages to Admiral Rockwell informing him of the current situation and requested the need for two more reserve battalions. In one of the reports he wrote, "Evidence of greater enemy strength than anticipated. Indication of lack of sufficient force to accomplish mission." He received no replies to his communications because the radio signals were broken up due to the harsh Aleutian weather.

Meanwhile, Vice Admiral Thomas Kinkaid, Commander of "Operation Landgrab," was hundreds of miles away on Adak Island and never met General Brown. He relied on Admiral Rockwell who was off the coast of Attu to provide him with reports on how the battle on Attu was going from reports from General Brown. General Brown's only report to Admiral Rockwell was aboard the USS Pennsylvania to report that the resupply route up Massacre Valley was exposed to Japanese fire and that the units at the head of the valley were suffering from the lack of supplies. Road-building equipment is needed so that vehicles could move supplies more quickly. It would also quicken the evacuation of the wounded which now takes up to two days and requires a stretcher party of eight. He emphasized that the troops were exhausted and fatigued by the constant resistance of the Japanese and the operational environment, and therefore requested additional troops. Admiral Rockwell agreed and forwarded that report on to Admiral Kinkaid who was not pleased with the "unsatisfactory progress."

Two days later subsequent reports by Brown which detailed out his assessment of the situations on the battlefield with its successes, failures, and shortcomings was sent by aircraft to Admiral Rockwell, but he never received them. The reason was because the dispatch aircraft carrying those reports crashed into the sea, and no one knew of its disappearance. Not receiving any reports, Admirals Rockwell and Kinkaid felt that Brown didn't want them to know how the ground forces were doing because the battle must have been going badly. This seemed logical because Brown had requested more troops, supplies, and weaponry than originally estimated. He also requested a 60-day supply of fuel and construction supplies for the Engineering Company. The Admirals were also wondering why the battle was taking so long since Brown claimed it would only take 3 days. Lieutenant Generals Buckner and Dewitt who disliked Brown were back on Adak Island with Admiral Kinkaid. General Dewitt speaks his mind, “Thomas, if Brown lacks aggressiveness he should be replaced.” General Buckner piles on, “I don't think that Brown understands the Aleutian environment. I think Major General Eugene Landrum should replace Brown.” “Let me review Landrum's military record and of another General that I think will be an excellent replacement.” After reviewing the generals' records, Admiral Kinkaid makes his decision, “I'm going to relieve Major General Brown of command and Major General Eugene Landrum will assume command starting on the 16th of May.”

General Landrum came ashore on Attu Island from Adak on a PBY and quickly met with the divisional staff at headquarters on the shore of Lake Elwood and was briefed on the current situation. He was surprised to learn that the Northern Force was assaulting the ridges on the east and west arms of Holtz Bay, and that the 2nd Battalion, 32nd Infantry supported by Company F of the 2nd Battalion, 17th Infantry was trying to seize the Massacre-Holtz Pass. General Landrum did not change any of Brown's plan nor did he alter the tactical and strategic force arrays. He even kept open Brown's request for additional troops, supplies, and other warfare assets.

Chapter 10
Holtz Bay and Massacre-Sarana Pass Secured

When Captain Bjork and his men got to the struggling Company C of the 2nd Battalion, 32nd Infantry Regiment, he saw that they were pinned down by the 270-man 6th Independent Mountain Artillery Company, under the command of Lieutenant Tairo Endo, that were armed with six Type 41 75-millimeter light howitzers. He quickly met with Captain Goodfellow who told hm, “Captain Bjork, glad to see you and your men. It looks like an artillery company snuck up on us after we secured the pass east of Massacre Valley.” “I got here as quickly as possible. My men are a bit tired because we just wiped out a company of Japs, but we're fit to kill as many Japs as we can.” “We have taken heavy casualties, the men are suffering from exposure, and are running low on ammo and supplies.” “We too are low, especially on ammo.” “I have a call in to the 21st Bombardment Squadron to parachute 2 loads of ammo and supplies down to us, and they are on their way now that the skies are somewhat clear. We have a couple of cases of ammo that you can have. I'll have some of my men bring them over to your men.” “Thanks” “Company B from my battalion is on the way to, so I need you and your men to take Hogback Ridge to block the Japanese at Massacre-Sarana Pass from receiving reinforcements.” “My men are up the task. I'll radio you when we secure Hogback Ridge.” “Good luck.”

When Captain Bjork got back to his company, he sees in the mixed cloudy skies, six B-24s from the 21st Bombardment Squadron dropping sixteen 100-pound general purpose bombs over the Japanese positions, followed by six B-25s dropping twelve 300-pound general purpose bombs. Lieutenant Fong is glad to see

Captain Bjork, “Captain, what is our next assignment.” “We have to take Hogback Ridge to keep Japanese reinforcements from reaching their men at Massacre-Sarana Pass. But first some men from the 32nd are bringing us a couple of cases of ammo, and then we'll be on our way.”

After the men of Company F were resupplied with ammunition, they turned to climb up the frigid terrain towards Hogback Ridge. The climb was made difficult due to the remaining winter snow on the ground which made their clothing and leather boots even more wet. Many of the men were starting to get trench foot and frostbite on their hands. When Captain Bjork and his men reached Hogback Ridge, it was absent of Japanese soldiers. After it was secured, ten of the men complained to their lieutenants that they were no longer fit to fight because their feet were numb, swollen and turning blue. Captain Bjork agreed to let them go back to the base hospital because he knew that they would be a liability to the company. The rest of men were ordered to set up a defense of the ridge and keep alert for any approaching Japanese soldiers.

****

Lieutenant Tairo's 4th company of the 6th Independent Mountain Artillery Company who was defending the 500-foot high Massacre-Sarana Pass, gets a call from First Lieutenant Toshio Hayashi of the 1st Company of the 303rd Infantry over at Massacre Valley Pass that he is sending a platoon of his soldiers over to reinforce his unit by way of Hogback Ridge. Lieutenant Hayashi calls his 2nd lieutenant over, “Lieutenant Nishimura, take your platoon over to Tairo's 4th company at Massacre-Sarana Pass. They're in need of reinforcements badly because they are having a hard time keeping the Americans at bay. They say that they are being bombed from the air. Give Sergeant Majors Hirano and Ono two of our Type 99 Nambu light machine guns and hurry." "Yes sir!"

****

Corporal Evans of Company F who is the forward lookout on the east side of Hogback Ridge comes running back to warn Captain Bjork that a platoon of Japanese soldiers are heading towards them. "Captain Bjork, it looks like a platoon strength of Japanese are coming our way. It looks like they are about a mile away." "It must be reinforcements from the 303rd soldiers over at Massacre Valley Pass. Get back to your look out station and let me know when they get within 500 yards of us or when they spot us." "Yes sir" "Lieutenant Fong, set up an 'Engage and Envelop Defense' towards those Japs, and get platoon A into those trenches, place platoon B parallel to the pass on the north side, platoon C parallel to the pass on the south side, and platoons D, E and F on the upper ridges above us. Put two BAR's with bipods up there too. Tell the men to hold their fire until I blow my whistle." Lieutenant Fong gathers his men and gives each platoon their assignments. Corporal Evens runs back again, "Japs are a quarter of a mile away and they have spotted us. I don't think they can see that we are company strength and outnumber them because they are preparing to attack and mounting their bayonets." Captain Bjork yells to his men, "The Japs are coming to us. Commence firing when I blow my whistle."

As the Japanese platoon led by Lieutenant Nishimura with his sword in his left hand and a grenade in his right hand, rushed towards Hogback Ridge firing their rifles and machine guns screaming "banzai, banzai, banzai."

Captain Bjork blows his whistle, "Tweeeet, tweeeet." Nishimura throws his grenade that kills two soldiers from Platoon B as he is hit with tens of bullets. Suddenly a rain of bullets pours down on the Japanese from the front, the right, the left, and from above. American and Japanese hand grenades are thrown and exploding in all directions. One by one the Japanese soldiers fall to the ground, some still firing their rifles, and killing and wounding American soldiers before they die. The air is filled with smoke from hundreds of rifle fire and tens of grenade blasts. It took no more than 3 minutes to shoot and kill the outnumbered Japanese platoon from the 303rd Infantry. Fifty-six Japanese soldiers lay dead in pools of blood. Lieutenant Ricci walks over to pick Nishimura's sword for a souvenir of the fire fight. Colonel Yamaski's Regiment of 2,500 men was quickly diminishing, but so was Captain Bjork's Company F of the 2nd Battalion, 17th Light Infantry Regiment, 7th Army Division. Because Company F had a 4 to 1 soldier and position advantage, it only loss 9 men killed, 10 seriously wounded, 3 with minor wounds, and 4 suffering debilitating pain from swollen and numb feet that were turning blue.

****

The following day at the ridges over looking Holtz Bay, the Northern Force was assaulting the Japaneses soldiers of the 2nd Sector dug into the ridge above. First Lieutenant "Wild Bill" Davis, leading the men of Company B, 1st Battalion, 17th Infantry, found a covered approach on the northern end of the ridge which allowed the company to climb the steep slope on the right flank of the Japanese giving them a dominate position on the high ground. The rest of the 1st Battalion moved to the top of the north end of the ridge and called in air support.

Sixteen wildcats from the Nassau Aircraft Carrier made strafing runs over the Japanese dug in on the ridge between the east and west arms of Holtz Bay

The 1st Battalion held their positions and waited for the rest of the 32nd Regiment to arrive. On May 17th, Colonel Culin and the men of the 32nd Regiment arrived at the ridge and waited to decide which of his battalions would lead the attack on the Japanese. Colonel Culin finally picked the 3rd Battalion. Lieutenant Colonel Finn, the commanding officer of the 3rd Battalion launched the attack shortly after midnight. His men reached the top of the ridge at 0300 hours only to find that Lieutenant Colonel Hiroshi Yonekawa and his men of the North Kuril Island Fortress Infantry had retreated to the ridges on the east arm of Holtz Bay and Fish Hook ridges. They also abandoned the area around Holtz Bay and left so quickly that they left behind a large store of supplies and equipment including their artillery guns.

****

When the Japanese retreated from ridges on the arms of Holtz Bay, Colonel Yamasaki called in his two top officers for a strategy meeting. "Lieutenant Colonel Yonekawa and Major Seiji Aota, I called you in to say that because we lost control of the ridge between the east and west arms Holtz Bay area, we're forced to wage a battle of attrition against the Americans from the high grounds. We've lost a third of our regiment, armaments, and supplies. Our food supply is so low that I'm ordering one meal a day. By retreating to the upper snowy ridges where we will have superior fields of fire and unimpeded vantage points. If we can hold off the Americans for 10 more days a naval fleet is coming to rescue us. A message from Vice Admiral Nobutake Kondo of the Imperial Navy at Tokyo Bay is sending a fleet of four carriers, three battleships, and eleven destroyers to rescue us. He says it will take a week and a half for the fleet to sail to Attu Island." Major Aota questions Yamasaki, "I think it is a false message to fool the Americans. One of the captains from the submarines that brought us our supplies last month told me that the Navy loss four of our carriers at Midway and does not have that many ships left in our navy. I believe that the navy can not tell us that it is a false message so that the Americans will think that it is true." "Aota, I think you are right that the message is false, but don't tell the men. Just pass the word along to all our units that we're moving our defenses to the high grounds and that we have to hold off the Americans for 10 days because a navy task force is coming to rescue us. We have to raise the morale of our men." Lieutenant Yonekawa concurs, "Yes, some of my men are breaking under the stress of battle, they are cold and hungry. Ordering one meal a day of one bowl of rice is going to really demoralize them. Some have even ran alone firing at the Americans so that they could kill them and put them out of their misery." "Well, we don't have any options left to survive as long as we can. So like I said, pass the word along to all your units that we're moving up to the upper parts of the mountains immediately. Start building defenses over Massacre-Sarana Pass, Chichagof Harbor, the East Arm of Holtz Bay, Cold Mountain, and the ridges overlooking Lake Nichols."

****

It is now May 19th, the eighth day of fighting on Attu Island and the Americans are suffering cold weather injuries at an alarming rate. The ice, fog, wind, and snow have inflicted twice as many injuries than from the Japanese. The 2nd Battalion, 17th Infantry Regiment was ordered to return to Massacre-Sarana Pass to help the 1st and 2nd Battalion, 32nd Infantry to defeat the Japanese at Massacre-Sarana pass which is 800 feet over sea level. Captain Bjork has a briefing with his Lieutenants before getting the orders to attack. "I don't have to tell you that this assignment is going to be a bastard. The skies are clear today and the Japs will have a clear view of us coming up the mountain. Fong, I want your platoon to fire the 81-millimeter mortar smoke rounds to mask the attack just before platoons C, D and F charge up the mountain. Sergeant Richards you will lead platoon C and Lieutenant Reynolds your platoon will take the center of the charge, Ricci, your platoon will take the left flank and Atwood, you will take the right flank. We should get the signal to attack in about 20 minutes so give the men instructions on what to do." Fong talks to Ricci and Atwood. "Hey guys, I wanted to lead the center of the advance so we could all be together to take on the Nips. That way we could watch over each other's platoon. I begged Bjork to let me be the center and have Platoon C fire those smoke shell. I'm pissed. Anyway, you guys watch your asses, you know the Nips always look to shoot the officers first." Atwood pats Fong on the back, "Albert don't worry about us. Just keep firing those smoke shells ahead of us so those Japs can't see us coming" Ricci interjects, "Don't worry Albert, Charlie and I have mud all over our lieutenant insignias so those slant-eyed Japs can't see if we're officers." "Okay, let's get back to our platoons and give the Nips hell. I'll be right after you guys once my platoon stops firing the smoke shells."

At 0930, the signal to was given and Lieutenant Fong give the orders to commence firing their mortar's smoke rounds to the top and below the ridges of the dugged-in Japanese which covers the movements of the advancing Company F. Even though the Japanese can't see that well, they can hear the bullets and artillery shells coming towards them. Initially the Japanese mistook the smoke for poison gas and frantically put on their gas masks.

As confusion rains over the Japanese, B-24 bombers from the 36th Bombardment Squadron drop forty 100-pound bombs on Chichagof. The B-25 bombers from the 73rd Bombardment squadron and 77th Bombardment Squadron drop thirty 300-pound general purpose bombs on the ridges between Bassett Creek and Lake Nichols in support of the Americans attacking at Massacre-Sarana Pass. The bombings were followed by jets from the 54th Fighter Squadron that strafed any Japanese that they could see from the air. It didn't take long for the Americans to force the Japanese to retreat up into the mountains above Massacre-Sarana Pass and build strongholds in the upper mountains. Atop a precipitous 1700-foot mountain ridge, Lieutenant Hitoshi Honna with 50 survivors of his 2nd Company, 303rd Infantry Regiment, built a strong defense around three Nambu Type 92 Heavy Machine guns mounted on tripods.

The next day, Lieutenant Harry Gilbert led his Company G, 2nd Battalion, 32nd Infantry up that snow covered 45-degree slopes. After only 30 minutes of fighting, Company G suffered casualties of 15%. After Lieutenant Gilbert was shot and killed, Company G retreated carrying their dead commanding officer back down the mountain. Major Charles Fredericks, Commander of the 2nd Battalion was beside himself with anger over the death of Lieutenant Gilbert and called for Captain Harvey Stevenson of Company E and Sergeant First Class Tidwell of Company G. “I called you in to tell you how upset I am over the loss of Lieutenant Gilbert and the many casualties of Company G. To claw up that steep incline to the Japanese forces on top of that ridge during the day is way too dangerous. Our second attempt to take out that Japanese stronghold is to do it at night. I've chosen your company Captain Stevenson for that assignment and I want Sergeant Tidwell to accompany you so he can help you navigate that steep 45-degree slope. His squad made it halfway before they had to retreat. Tidwell what did you learn?" "Well there is a covered shelf on the left side that I found and it can protect us until we get within 40 yards from their machine gun nests. When they stopped firing their machine guns, I could hear those Japs calling us derisive words in English. Like, 'Come and get us you fucking round-eyes' and 'Die you Yankee sons-of-bitchees.' I tried to shoot those guys, but I missed. But they missed me too." Captain Stevenson inquires, "What time tonight do you want us to go?" "At 0000 hours when the night turns really dark and the clouds block out the moonlight is when you should go. They will have some watch guards up, but if you can take them out quickly before the others wake-up and get to those machine guns, you should be able to neutralize them." "Sounds good to me sir. I'll tell my men to get some sleep before we go at midnight."

Captain Stevenson and Company E executed their night attack as planned and quietly climb up the steep covered slope under the guidance of Sergeant Tidwell. When they got close to the enemy's camp, they were ordered to mount their bayonets. When they got within 30 yards of the closest machine gun nest, Tidwell threw a grenade into it. The explosion alerted the watch guards and fired their rifles at the advancing Americans. Many of the awakened Japanese soldiers came rushing out of their tents firing wildly in to the night, only to be killed by a barrage of bullets from the onrushing men of Company E. Hand-grenades were thrown into the second and third machine-gun nests before they could be turned and fired. A screaming Lieutenant Honna came rushing towards the Americans firing his pistol killing two Yankee Joes before Sergeant Tidwell saw him and fired a burst of bullets from his BAR that almost cut Honna's body in half. The Japanese who ran out of their rifle bullets charged the Americans with their bayonets screaming "Tenno Heika Banzai," or "Long live the Emperor." Some of them were able to impale and kill 4 men of Company E with their bayonets before all of the Japanese soldiers of the 2nd Company were killed while Company E sustained very low casualties of their own.

****

Back at Company F, 2nd Battalion, 17th Infantry, after 8 days of battling a tenacious Japanese Regiment in the most grim and forbidding weather on earth, all the men were suffering from either battle fatigue, frostbite, trench foot, wet clothing, and hypothermia or a variable combination of all those afflictions. The temperature on Attu since the fighting began rarely went above 40 degrees Fahrenheit. Company F was now down to 156 men and 5 officers. Benefiting from the clothing mistakes made by the generals on the First Attacking Forces, the combat and support troops who came ashore after them were better equipped to handle the cold because of better boots and clothing. When Company F came upon dead soldiers who wore those better clothes and boots, they were conflicted about taking those boots, jackets, and parkas. Captain Bjork decides to approve the stripping off the better clothes and boots of the dead soldier to improve the survival chances of his men. Lieutenants Fong, Ricci, Atwood, Hahn, and Reynolds are ambivalent. Albert voices his opinion, "We know that we need warmer clothes and dryer boots, but taking them off our dead soldiers doesn't seem right to me." Tony answers, "Albert, we were issued the crummy clothes and leather boots while the back-up reserves were issued the warmer clothes and water-proof boots. Those guys are dead and they don't need them anymore." Charlie agrees, "It's not like we're stealing from the dead, just think that they are happy to donate their clothes to us so we can be dryer and warmer." Lieutenant Reynolds concurs, "The thought of stripping off their clothes and boots leaving them in just their underwear is repugnant to me, but our men need better clothing." Lieutenant Hahn mumbles, "I could use a warmer Jacket and pair of boots as long as the fit." Albert capitulates, "Okay, we'll let the men know that it is okay to strip the better jackets, parkas, pants, socks and boots of our dead soldiers. But, tell them that if they find any personal items in their clothing like letters from or to home, pictures of their family, or girlfriend, to stuff them in the dead soldier's underwear. Also, tell them that when they remove any clothing off the dead soldiers to make sure that their dog-tags remain around their necks so the medics will know who they are."

Chapter 11
The Men of the 3rd Battalion, 17th Infantry

On May 20th, Colonel Wayne C. Zimmerman, who was the Regimental Commander of the 17th Infantry Regiment (Assault Force) ordered his 3rd Battalion, which was badly mauled at the Massacre-Holtz Bay Pass, to take Sarana Nose which was a ridgeline jutting out from the east towards Lake Nichols. That ridge dominated the narrow entrance of the valley leading into Chicagof Harbor. On Sarana Nose was Major Tokuji Watanabe in charge of the Chichagof Harbor Sector with the remnants of his 664-man 303rd Independent Infantry Battalion. Watanabe seeing that the Americans are building massive forces again him, called his three remaining officers together to go over their defense. "Lieutenant Okazaki, how many men are still left in our Battalion?" "We have 429 left, but many are badly wounded, but capable of fighting" "Lieutenant Furuta, where do you think the Americans will be attacking us from?" "They will probably come from the east sector because I see that they are setting up heavy artillery units there." "Lieutenant Haruyama move your men from the western section and split then up on the flanks of the eastern sector. It's getting dark now and they won't be attacking at night because their artillery won't be able to fix coordinates on us, I think they will be coming in the morning, but still set up watch guards around the perimeter of our defense tonight."

****

Down at field headquarters, Colonel Zimmerman is meeting with his officers to go over the plan of attack on the 303rd Independent Infantry Battalion. "Lieutenant

Colonel Fish, you will lead the attack tomorrow morning at 0630 hours. The 48th and 49th Artillery Batteries on the east side will start firing their cannons, and the 78th Coast Artillery Battery will shell the Japanese from the south. They will continue firing until you get within 50 yards of the Sarana Nose ridgeline. When you reach that point, radio me and we'll cease fire. After we stop shelling, because we don't want any friendly-fire killings, you can start your attack on the Japanese." "Which two companies did you select to be in the attacking force?" "Lieutenant Redmond of I Company and Lieutenant McCoin of L Company, I selected your companies because they are the strongest of our four companies. Your men should easily take out those Japanese after the artillery softens them up."

At exactly 0630 hours the next morning, fourteen 37-millimeter anti-tank guns, twenty-three 81-millimeter mortars, four 75-millimeter pack howitzers, and four batteries of 105-millimeter howitzers opened fire on the Japanese devastating their stronghold. When Lieutenant Colonel Fish radioed in to cease fire, his men quickly rushed up the ridge to kill all of the dazed and wounded Japanese soldiers of the 303rd Infantry. Major Watanabe was killed by an artillery blast while the Americans suffered minor casualties.

After Colonel Zimmerman's victory at Sarana Nose Ridge, he mobilized the 2nd Battalion, 32nd Infantry (Reserve Force) to take on the dug-in Japanese high up on Fish Hook and Buffalo Ridges that overlooked the valley floor and the Chichagof Harbor. He had the artillery batteries moved over to those ridges and had them set up in a similar pattern as the one at Sarana Nose. He selected Companies G and H to lead the assault. On May 20th at 1645 hours, the batteries of the 78th, 48th and 49th Artillery companies battered the Japanese out of their machine gun nests and bunker hideaways leaving little resistance to the on coming Americans that made it easy for Companies G and H to overcome the Japanese.

With two victories in two days over the Japanese, Colonel Zimmerman was feeling invincible and ordered the 2nd Battalion, 17th Light Infantry Regiment to attack the Machine Gun Company under the command of First Lieutenant Yu Kato situated above Holtz-Chichagof Pass. Major Smith the CO of the 2nd Battalion ordered Captain Bjork of Company F to be the point company to lead the attack and Captain Staab of Company E to be the backup reserve. He then assigned Lieutenant Washnok to lead Company G because Captain Jones was wounded in action. Company G was assigned to cover Company F's left flank, and for Captain Womack of Company H to protect Company F's right flank.

After Company F received word that they were to be the point company to lead the attack on the Japanese Machine Gun Company, the five lieutenants sat in 1st Lieutenant Fong's tent to talk about how the battle on Attu Island was going. Albert opens the conversation, “Tomorrow's attack on the Nips is going to be ugly. They are protected in rocky trenches and caves with connecting tunnels. The top of this mountain is always surrounded by clouds and that is why the bomber squadrons haven't been able fly over it. Charlie agrees, “I don't know about you guys, but I have a bad feeling about this assignment. I just wrote a letter to my mom and dad about this hell hole of an island and if I don't come back that I truly loved them for being the best parents a son could ask for. You guys should send a letter to your families to say how you're doing and that you miss them.” Tony adds, “I'm going to write home and to Carol after this battle on this island is over. We're not able to get letters or mail our letters out while we're fighting Japs on the battle fields.

Albert says, "I sent a letter to my family just before D-Day and told them how wet and rainy Attu Island is and that I might catch a cold because we weren't issued arctic weather clothing. I was able to mail it, so they should have gotten it by now." Tony laughs, "Albert, you crack me up. We'll all be lucky if we get out of this war with nothing worse than a cold." Charlie grins, "I hope you're right Tony, but if I get killed, make sure that my letter gets mailed to my parents." Albert admonishes Charlie, "Don't say or even think that. As long as were together, we'll all get back home alive." Lieutenant Hahn adds, "For me, I would rather be killed, than to come back from the war as a quadriplegic." Lieutenant Reynolds speaks up, "Okay guys, let's not anguish over the talk of death and dismemberment and be positive about getting through this war alive. Negative thoughts bring about negative results." Lieutenant Fong agrees, "Lieutenant Reynolds is veracious, we have to be positive. Let's get back to our platoons and prepare them for tomorrow's fight."

On the early morning of May 23rd, the skies over Holtz-Chichagof Pass are free of clouds, so Major Smith places calls into the 36th Bombardment Squadron to send their B-24s to carpet bomb the Machine Gun Company on Holtz-Chichagof Pass before he orders his 2nd Battalion to attack the Japanese. It only took 30 minutes for five B-24 bombers to fly over the Japanese positions with each bomber dropping ten 100-pound general purpose bombs and ten 120-pound fragmentation bombs. The bombings demolished half of the machine gun nests and a third of the Machine Gun Company's soldiers.

With the Japanese in total disarray by the unexpected bombings, Major Smith gave the order for the 2nd Battalion to attack. As the Americans closed in near the Japanese, they are hit by fire from two machine gun nests and hand grenades. Lieutenant Atwood's platoon quickly fans out retuning fire and throwing hand grenades of their own. Atwood throws a hand grenade into one of the machine gun nests, demolishing it, and runs forward firing in his Colt .45 pistol. As he stops to reload, he is shot in the chest and falls backward onto the muddy dirt and snowy tundra.

Lieutenant Fong's platoon is hit with a mortar shell, but it doesn't explode. Ten of his men have fallen from Japanese fire. Fong fires an M1 rifle he picked up from one of his fallen men shooting a Japanese soldier before he can throw his hand-grenade. Since the Japanese occupy the high position, Fong's platoon was not able to break through the center of the Japanese front and are driven back one by one. Lieutenant Reynolds' platoon is taking heavy casualties, and retreating under fire from a Type 92 heavy machine gun and fire from a Type 99 light machine gun. Reynolds is wounded in this right arm, but is still able to stumble down the mountain to safety. Lieutenant Ricci's platoon is taking light casualties, but he sees the other platoons are being driven back and retreats back and regroups with the other platoons of Company F. After the battle, Lieutenants Fong and Ricci were told that Lieutenant Atwood was shot and killed. They were taken over to see the body of their best friend and fellow officer. Albert falls to his knees and cradles Charlie in his arms. “Hey, you're not suppose to die damn it.” Tony shaking his head in grief, “Poor Charlie, he shouldn't have talked about dying in that letter to his parents. It must have brought him bad luck. I'll find that letter and make sure it gets mailed. Goddamned Japs. I hate them more than ever.” Captain Bjork comes over, “Shit, It pains me to see any of my men get killed whether he is a private or an officer. Atwood was a fine and intelligent lieutenant. He did his duty and never complained to me about this godforsaken Island. I know how you and Atwood were best of friends, Fong and Ricci you can carry lieutenant Atwood down to the hospital morgue and see that he gets a proper burial in the temporary cemetery. Also take Lieutenant Reynolds to the hospital too. He is badly wounded in his right arm and is unable to use it." Lieutenant Ricci replies, "Thanks Captain Bjork. We'll met you back at the bivouac area in about an hour or two."

The 3rd Battalion, 32nd Infantry, which had come up from Holtz Bay set up a defensive position on the east arm of Holtz Bay Ridge and waited in reserve. On May 24th at 0100 hours, a reinforced platoon combat patrol was sent into the Holtz-Sarana Pass and destroyed three machine gun positions and then retreated back to its company. Another battalion patrol in the morning strung a telephone wire between the command post of the 32nd Battalion and the command post of the 2nd Battalion, 17th Infantry regiment, establishing direct communications between the Southern and Northern Forces.

Chapter 12
Dulce et Decorum est Pro Patria Mori

As Captain Bjork surveys the rows of dead 2nd Battalion, 17th Light Infantry Regiment soldiers that total 30, he thinks of the Roman poet Horace who wrote, “It is sweet and proper to die for one's country.” He questions if his men felt sweet and proper as they were taking their last breath. He grieves as he shakes his head and mumbles to himself, “I don't think so.” He turns away from the sight of his dead fellow comrades and heads back to his bivouac camp at the base of Holtz-Chichagof Pass ridge to await his next order to kill more Japanese soldiers.

On May 24th, General Landrum ordered the 2nd Battalion, 17th Infantry from the Southern Force and the 1st Battalion, 32, Infantry form the Northern force to attack and seize the Holtz Bay-Chichagof Harbor Pass. It didn't take long for the 2nd Battalion to join up with the 1st Battalion although they were still fatigued, cold and short of men because of the battlefield fight the day before. Major Smith rested his men for several hours before the Americans launched their attack. At 1200 hours, the 2nd Battalion advanced up the southern slopes of the ridge, while the 1st Battalion worked its way up the northern slopes. Company F, 2nd Battalion encountered heavy Japanese machine gun fire. Lieutenant Ricci ordered his platoon to take cover and return fire. His BAR rifleman, Sergeant Barge, who was next to him was shot in the right shoulder and dropped his browning automatic rifle. Ricci immediately picked up the BAR and fired it at the Japanese machine gun nest, yelling at the top of his lungs, “This is for Charlie you dammed bastards.” He kept firing until he ran out of bullets. As he reached over to get more .30-06 cartridges from Sergeant Barge, Lieutenant Ricci was hit by rifle fire in the head and killed instantly. His men picked up their lieutenant and were forced back to their lines of departure.

While platoon E, Company F was retreating, Lieutenants Fong's platoon A and Lieutenant Hahn's platoons F were pinned down by fire from three machine gun nests. Both platoons tried to inch their way up the ridges to throw hand grenades, but were never able to get within fifty yards of the those nests. Luckily there were several ditches that the platoons were able to shelter themselves in from the rain of bullets from the Japanese. Captain Bjork realized that it was suicidal to get close enough to use their hand grenades, so he ordered his men to retreat back to the base camp because enough of his men were killed or wounded. As the rest of Company F's platoons were moving quickly down the ridges, Lieutenant Hahn was shot in his left hip and tumbled to the ground. His men picked him up and were able to carry him to safety. As company F, 2nd Battalion, regrouped to calculated their casualty count, they were stunned to learn that Lieutenant Ricci was killed, Lieutenant Hahn was seriously wounded, 9 men were killed, 10 men were seriously wounded that required hospitalization and 3 had painful trench foot.

When 1st Lieutenant Fong saw the dead body of Tony with half of his head blown off, he choked up with several tears slowly rolling down his right cheek and held Tony's left hand. “Not you too Tony. Shit, you were suppose to have a big wedding, and I was going to be your best man.” Albert could not look at Tony's bullet shattered head with blood and part of his brain still dripping from his head any longer and slowly walked away with several tears slowly rolling down his left cheek. Company F, 2nd Battalion, 17th Light Infantry Regiment was now down to 116 men. The 1st Battalion also was driven back off the northern slope with heavy casualties. The day ended with the 1st Battalion, 4th Infantry successfully getting two companies into the Holtz Bay side of the Holtz-Sarana Pass.

Although the 2nd and 1st Battalions were forced to retreat, the day was positive for the Air Force when the clouds and fog cleared away which allowed the Eleventh Air Force to send six B-24s and five B-25s to drop 16 tons of bombs on the Japanese in Chichagof Harbor. One bomber group accidentally dropped bombs near the 2nd Battalion, 32nd Infantry area, but no Americans were injured.

In preparations for the attack on Fish Hook Ridge 105-millimeter guns were dragged up the newly built road in Massacre Valley, but a small ridge prevented them from making direct sightings on Fish Hook Ridge. However, they were within range to fire over the ridge to hit the Japanese on Fish Hook Ridge. A group of soldiers was able to drag by ropes a 37-millimeter howitzer over the small ridge to where it could make direct fire on the Japanese when the Americans start their attack.

The night was cold and frigid as the battalions of 17th and 32nd prepared for the attack the next day. At Company F, 2nd Battalion, 17th Infantry, Captain Bjork and 1st Lieutenant Fong were meeting to go over the plan of attack on Fish Hook Ridge. "Lieutenant Fong you are the last of my six lieutenants, so you and I will lead Company F, and a reduced platoon from Company G led by Lieutenant Little, up Fish Hook Ridge tomorrow. I think we are at an altitude of over 2,000 feet and it is freezing cold and windy out there. The taking of Fish Hook Ridge will isolate the remaining Japanese Garrison to the Chichagof Harbor and Attu Village. Once we do that, Yamasaki will be boxed in and will have to surrender. The Japanese have several well-placed light and heavy machine guns, so digging them out is going to be a Herculean Task." "I can't wait to get off this cold and hellhole of an island. I know once we defeat the Japanese and retake Attu, the 7th Division Army will be sent to the Pacific Islands to fight the Japanese over there. Fighting in the warm tropical sun will be like a picnic compared to this goddamned island. Oh, when we get off Attu, I going to have to mail Charlie's letter to his parents. Wish Tony wrote a letter to his dad and to his fiancé Carol." "Lieutenant Fong, I must tell you that you are the finest 1st lieutenant that I ever served with. Okay, get a good sleep and I'll see you early tomorrow morning." "Goodnight Captain."

On May 25th at 1000 hours, air strikes and artillery supported the assault on Fish Hook Ridge. The 2nd Battalion, 17th Infantry and the 1st Battalion, 4th Infantry successfully took the 2,100 foot peak overlooking Fish Hook Pass. The 3rd Battalion, 32nd Infantry was pinned down by heavy machine gun fire and could not advance any further. As G Company, 2nd Battalion was advancing high up on Fish Hook Ridge, F Company, 2nd Battalion move forward to assist. When both companies G and F reached the ridge at 2,300 feet, Captain Bjork gave 1st Lieutenant Fong an order., "Fong organize an attack with with forces that are available. Take a platoon from our company and have Lieutenant Little take a platoon from his company and attack the saddle and clear a path down to Chichagof Harbor and Attu Village." Lieutenants Fong and Little formed platoons from the most available and closest men round them, and quickly led them along a steep and rocky terrain at an altitude of over 2,400 feet. "Little take your platoon and hit their stronghold from the top side and I'll take them from the side. As they attacked the stronghold, both platoons faced heavy machine gun fire. Fong began firing his M1 rifle hitting the ground as he threw a hand grenade, but it fell short of the machine gun nest. As he stood up again to throw another hand grenade, he was hit by rifle fire in the leg and then in the chest throwing him to the ground as he took his last breath. Lieutenant Little knew they were in a losing position and called the men to retreat back down the saddle while he rushed over to see if Fong was still alive so that he could pull him to safety. As he was nearing Fong's body, Lieutenant Little was shot and killed as he fell off into a ravine.

When the retreating platoons from F and G Companies got back down off Fish Hook Ridge, they reported to Captain Bjork that Lieutenants Fong, Little, and 5 men got killed, not counting the wounded on their failed assault on the Japanese. Bjork asked how and where the lieutenants were killed, and after they told him, he walked away without saying a word and reloaded his Colt .45. Captain Bjork was inconsolable and heartbroken about the killing of 1st Lieutenant Fong and told his men that he was going up to the saddle, risking his life to retrieve Fong's body. Several of his men volunteered to go with him, but he said being alone he had a better chance of slipping by the Japanese without being seen. Then he quickly and stealthy reached the saddle unseen. He slowly crawled on his hands and knees and was able to retrieve Fong's body and carried it back down the mountain. The medics took the 1st lieutenant's body to the morgue while Captain Bjork was resolute in wanting to kill more Japanese soldiers, especially the ones that killed 1st Lieutenant Fong. He got his chance when the 1st and 2nd Battalions regrouped and were ordered to make a second attempt to take Fish Hook Ridge the next day.

Meanwhile the 2nd Battalion, 32nd Infantry and the 3rd Battalion, 17th Infantry had resumed their assault on the Japanese firing down on them from Buffalo Ridge near the southern end of Lake Cories, but again they were halted. They needed help from the 77th Bombardment Squadron and they sent seven B-24s, eleven B-25s, and 20 P-38s to bomb and strafe those dug in Japanese.

All Americans were running short on food, supplies, and ammunition because the carrying parties were struggling to keep up with the demands and torturous terrain that required ropes to get those supplies up ridges. However, the Japanese were suffering more shortages

Chapter 13
An American Pyrrhic Victory

On the morning of May 26th, the 2nd Battalion, 17th Infantry and the 1st Battalion, 4th Infantry made a second attempt to dislodge the Japanese on Fish Hook Ridge. To secure the Peak and clear the way through the Holtz Bay-Chichagof Harbor Pass, the task was given to Company A, 1st Battalion, 17th Infantry and Lieutenant Colonel John "Mickey" Finn's 3rd Battalion, 32nd Infantry. By 0900 hours, they reached the 2,400 foot crest, but then they were stopped by Japanese machine gun, rifle, and grenade launcher fire. The Japanese fortifications blocked access to the Holtz-Chichagof Pass. Company K came within 150 feet of the top of the narrow pass, but was blocked by snow trenches filled with Japanese soldiers. Not dissuaded by those trenches, Private Joe Martinez stood up and waved others forward. He single handedly assaulted the trenches, firing his Browning Automatic Rifle and throwing his hand grenades. As he reached the top of the steep pass, he was shot in his head and mortally wounded. The men of Company K seeing Martinez's courage, rose up and assaulted the Japanese killing all of them and clearing the way so that they could advance on to Chichagof. As Company K moved on towards Chichagof, they came across two lost and dazed Japanese soldiers who wanted to surrender. They became the first POW's of the battle. When they were interrogated, they said that the Japanese were starving for food and running out of ammunition. After hearing this, General Landrum wanted to make a direct appeal to the remaining Japanese and had surrender leaflets printed.

Over the next two days the 11th Air force dispatched their B-24s, B-25s and P-38s on numerous bombing and strafing runs that supported the infantry to defeat the

Japanese and to chase them into their last stronghold in the mountain areas around Chichagof. Soon the American Forces dominated the high grounds around Chichagof. This was when a low flying PBY dropped surrender leaflets over Chichagof Harbor. The leaflets were addressed to Colonel Yamasaki from General Landrum which explained that he was in a hopeless situation and asked him and his men to surrender. The leaflets read:

Your attention is called to the fact that your forces are now in a hopeless position, and that because the United States forces control the air and sea lanes, there is no chance of reinforcements for your troops. Therefore, in accordance with the rules of land warfare, I ask for the unconditional surrender of the Japanese Garrison of Attu Island. Your defense and soldierly conduct of your troops have been worthy of the highest military traditions. It is requested that the Commanding Officer, accompanied by not to exceed four staff officers, proceed openly in broad daylight under white flags in a southerly direction in Chichagof Valley to the vicinity of the South End of Lake Cories. This party will not be fired upon and will be met by guides who will conduct you to the place where the surrender will be received. After the surrender, your forces will be entitled to and will receive all privileges due prisoners of war according to the rules of land warfare.

****

The thought of surrender was abhorrent to Colonel Yamasaki and to the code of Bushido which means, "the way of the warrior." To Yamasaki, even acknowledging the leaflets was unworthy of a warrior, and as such never replied in words, but in action. So on May 28, Colonel Yamasaki called all his units together, to discuss how they should respond to General Landrum's call to surrender. “Fellow soldiers, as all of you know our garrison is down to about 700 able men. We are trapped on all four sides of Chichagof Harbor. We have only three choices of action. We can retreat up to the high mountains to the east, stand and fight here at Chichagof, or to surprise attack them at Massacre Bay Beach.” Captain Jiro Tsuya of Headquarters, 2nd Sector voices his opinion, “Colonel, retreating back into the mountains is not an option because we have almost no food supplies left, and we would all starve to death within a week.” Major Masashi Aoto of the Anti-aircraft Artillery, 2nd Sector offers his choice. “If we stay here and fight, we can use our anti-aircraft and our heavy cannons against the Americans.” Colonel Yamasaki replies, “Staying here would be my second choice, but I think the Americans will not challenge us man to man. Instead they will use their bombers to drop hundreds of bombs to kill all of us while keeping their casualty rate low.” Captain Hiroyuki Numata of Headquarters, 2nd Sector says, “A surprise attack on the Americans at Massacre Bay is the choice for me if I have to die, I want to kill some 'Joes' before I die. This way I'll have a better chance to enter into Nirvana where there is Perfect Peace.” Yamasaki agrees, “Yes, if we surprise attack them at Massacre Bay Beach, they won't expect it. It is based with reserves and hospital units. They have stores of food and ammunition that we can capture and then we retreat back into the eastern mountains to fight for another two weeks until our re-enforcements arrive.” Captain Naojiro Oura of the North Sea Garrison Field Hospital comments, “If we do not succeed in our attack on Massacre Bay or if we retreat into the mountains with more food and ammo, the hundreds of sick and wounded men in the hospital units will be left to the Americans who will kill them.”

Yamasaki ponders, "Well in either case we can't let them be killed by the Americans, so Oura before we attack, have your doctors morphine the sick that can not kill themselves and have the wounded commit suicide with gun or grenade. So the choice of attacking is final. This is how we will line up for the attack. I want the 303rd to lead the attack on the left flank and the men of the Yonegawa Force on the right Flank. The remainder of the Army forces under command of Adjutant Captain Jiro Tsuya will form in the rear of the two infantry battalions as first and second reserve forces. The remaining naval forces will make up the third reserve force. We will attack in the early morning tomorrow, and if our attack is not looking successful, I will lead a Banzai charge instead." The men all shout, "Tenno Heika Banzai."

Early the next morning, Yamasaki gave the order to attack while the Americans were eating breakfast. The Japanese quietly marched through the narrow valley between Lake Cories and the lower slopes of Fish Hook ridge towards the slopes where the Army engineering units were based. A heavy fog concealed their advance. They first encountered Company B of a reserve unit which they smashed through the rear guard and killed many soldiers who were unarmed before they could defend themselves. They rushed on screaming as they caught the 3rd Battalion off guard, killing Lieutenant Colonel James Fish and Major Siddens of the 17th Infantry.

The objective of Colonel Yamasaki was to capture the artillery pieces on the top of the hill where the army engineers were based. If they could capture them, then he could use them to fire on the Americans. As they headed towards the hill where the engineers were, they came across an unguarded field hospital which was clearly marked with the International Red Cross. It was one of the 7th Medical Battalion's clearing companies with three tents in a row. Filled with hatefulness and uncontrolled rage, screaming “Banzai,” the Japanese soldiers threw hand grenades into the two outside tents, one of which caught fire with wounded American soldiers still inside. Then they went to the other tents and quickly killed the unarmed medics, doctors and other company personnel. With their bayonets they went cot to cot and killed all of the wounded soldiers, except for several soldiers who played dead laying on the ground.

Soon the 50th Engineers on top of a hill saw what was happening and quickly formed a defensive position as some 700 Japanese soldiers attacked them. As the engineers fired their rifles, killing many Japanese, the crest of the hill was breached, but the engineers stood fast and fought a hand-to-hand bloody fight until the Japanese were pushed back down the hill. Coming to the rescue were the 13th Engineers who reinforced the 50th. The Japanese regrouped at the bottom of the hill and Colonel Yamasaki ordered his men to attack the Americans again. This time, they didn't even make it to the crest of the hill, and retreated with hundreds of dead or dying Japanese lying on the hill. Yamasaki realizing that American infantry units would soon be arriving, ordered his remaining soldiers to commit “Jisatsu” or suicide. Within minutes, the open ground where the Japanese stood beaten and battered, reverberated with the sounds of exploding hand grenades, rifles shots, and screams of “Banzai, Banzai, Banzai.” Soon silence filled the air over some 450 dead Japanese soldiers that laid dead on the ground. Colonel Yamasaki was found with his sword in his hand.

****

After eighteen days of the most hellish fighting on Attu

Island, the Americans finally defeated the Japanese, but the cost was at the expense of 549 American dead, 1,148 wounded and about 2,100 suffering non-battle injuries and diseases. For the Americans in the Pacific War, the Battle of Attu Island had the second highest casualty rate after the Battle of Iwo Jima. For the Japanese, an estimated 2,351 were killed and 29 were prisoners of war.

If the number of casualties suffered by the victorious exceeds the casualty count of the defeated, it is considered a Pyrrhic Victory. The phrase dates back to Pyrrhus of Epirus, whose triumph against the Romans in the Battle of Asculum in 279 BC destroyed much of his forces, forcing the end of his campaign. Based on the American casualty count at Attu Island, can we not label the Battle of Attu Island a Pyrrhic Victory? Could this be the reason why the U.S. Army calls the Battle of Attu Island the "Forgotten Battle." Could this be why they wanted to forget about all the blunders and planning mistakes in preparing for their attack against the Japanese under operation "Landgrab" that resulted in the so many needless deaths of American soldiers?" Well at least the U.S. Army did learn a valuable lesson at Attu Island about cold weather amphibious landings and fighting suicidal Japanese soldiers. Those lessons helped the Americans in their amphibious landings against the Japanese in the battles fought in the Pacific Islands. However, those lessons were useless in their debacle to remove the Japanese garrison on Kiska Island.

On July 28, 1943, The Japanese Northern Army secretly evacuated its remaining garrison of 5,000 troops from the island of Kiska ending the Japanese occupation in the Aleutian Islands. It was inexplicable how military intelligence failed to realize that the Japanese had abandoned Kiska Island especially since aerial photograph analysts observed that the activities on the island decreased, and bomb damage was not being repaired anymore, and by July 28, no radio signals from Kiska were being detected. Ignoring these clues that the Japanese were no longer on the island, on the morning of August 15, 1943, with a heavy coastal barrage by an armada of nearly 100 allied warships, 34,000 American and Canadian combat infantrymen landed on Kiska Island under, "Operation Cottage," believing that 10,000 Japanese troops were fortified in the upper mountains of Kiska Island. The American U.S. 7th Infantry Division and 87th Mountain Infantry Regiment landed on one side of Kiska Island and the Canadian Fusiliers, the Winnipeg Grenadiers, the Rocky Mountain Rangers, and the Saint John Fusiliers landed on the opposite side of Kiska Island. After a day of searching for Japanese soldiers, none were found with the exception of stray dogs. Sadly, the next day both forces mistook the each other for the enemy and when a Canadian soldier fired at the Americans thinking they were Japanese, a sporadic friendly fire incident occurred, leaving 28 Americans and 4 Canadians dead, with 50 wounded on either side. Additional casualties occurred due to Japanese land mines, ammunition and vehicle accidents, and booby traps.

The destroyer USS Abner Read ran into a Japanese mine causing it to lose a large part of its stern. The blast killed 71 and wounded 47 sailors. All total, "Operation Cottage," which completed the Aleutian Islands campaign, caused the casualty list to rise to 92 killed, 221 wounded soldiers in addition to the 71 killed and 47 wounded sailors. Japanese casualties were zero. This was another lamentable operation of another battle that the American Army wanted to be "Forgotten" and unremembered in the history books of America. To save themselves from the embarrassment of what had happened, “Operation Cottage” was written off as a “Training Exercise.”

****

In 1987, The Japanese placed four memorials on the crest of Engineer Hill to honor all those who lost the lives in the Pacific during WWII. The largest is an 18-foot seven ton titanium star shaped “Peace Memorial” made by Sumitomo Metals Industry Ltd. The inscription reads:

In Memory of all Those Who Sacrificed
Their Lives in the Islands and
Seas of the North Pacific
And in Dedication to World Peace

Constructed by the Japanese Government of Japan
In Cooperation With
The Government of the United States
On 1 July 1987

Many veterans who fought on Attu were extremely upset about the Peace Memorial and were trying to get it removed because they felt that the Japanese were really trying to honor the 2,500 Japanese soldiers that died there.

The Americans to acknowledge Colonel Yamazaki's bravery erected two interpretive signs near where he fell near Engineering Hill. In 1950, the commander, 17th Naval District replaced one of them with a bronze plaque mounted on a stone foundation with the inscription, “Attu Island, World War II, 1943. Yamazaki, a Colonel in the Japanese Army, was killed in action near this point. Colonel Yamasaki commanded all Japanese troops on the Island.”

Afterword

In this historical novella just about all the American and Japanese officers and units were real. Also, most of the battles on the field actually took place. The main fictional characters were Charlie Atwood, Tony Ricci, and their families, girlfriends, and Albert's girlfriend Judee. Everything about Albert and his family is mostly true, especially how he was killed in action. Almost all reference documents and media information used in writing this novella, used the names of fallen American officers for peaks, valleys, and ridges where they were killed in action years after the Battle of Attu Island took place (see the list of those officers and soldiers on following pages). To keep my historical novella as true to the times that happened, I only used names of locations that existed at that time. For the ridges, valleys, passes, and peaks named after American officers and NCOs Killed in Actions (KIA), I just used just plain mountains, peaks, ridges, valleys or between or near existing named locations.

1st Lieutenant Albert Paul Fong

1st Lieutenant Albert Paul Fong was killed in action on May 25, 1943. He was 28 years old when he was killed. He was in the Army one year and nine months and was unmarried and had no children.

He was posthumously awarded the Silver Star for Gallantry on Attu Island. The Silver Star and Purple Heart were awarded to his father Mr. Fong Chow on Friday August 27, 1943, at the U.S. Army Replacement Depot in Pittsburgh, California. 1st Lieutenant Fong was also authorized the Asiatic Pacific Campaign Medal, the World War II Victory Medal, and the Combat Infantryman Badge. The medals were awarded by Colonel C.W. Jones in the name of the President of the United States.

Fong Chow was surrounded by his children Taft, Helen, Alice, Minnie, Marian, Martha, and Leslie.

1st Lieutenant Fong was initially buried at the Little Falls Military Cemetery on Attu Island in Massacre Valley. In 1948, all the U.S. dead were exhumed and interned at locations requested by their family or at the Sitka National Cemetery in Sitka, Alaska. 1st Lieutenant Fong was interned at Sunrise Memorial Cemetery, Vallejo, California at the request of his surviving family.

1st Lieutenant Fong's father passed away approximately one month prior to the return of his son. 1st Lieutenant Fong was also memorialized at his alma matter Springfield College dedicated to the dead from the Class of 1941.

Captain Delbert Leonard Bjork

The President of the United States of America, authorized by Act of Congress July 9, 1918, takes pleasure in presenting the Distinguished Service Cross to Captain (Infantry) Delbert L. Bjork, United States Army, for extraordinary heroism in connection with military operations against an armed enemy while serving with Company F, 17th Infantry Regiment, 7th Infantry Division, in action against enemy forces on 25 May 1943, at Attu, Territory of Alaska. Captain Bjork voluntarily lay in an exposed position in the face of withering fire by entrenched Japanese and directed fire that enabled other troops under his command to destroy the hostile position. **Later he penetrated enemy held territory to find one of his officers who had become a casualty.** Captain Bjork's outstanding leadership, personal bravery and zealous devotion to duty exemplify the highest traditions of the military forces of the United States of and reflect great credit upon himself, the 7th Infantry Division and the United States Army.

Before entering the service during World War II, Delbert Bjork was a professional American football offensive lineman in the National Football League and played two seasons for the Chicago Bears (1937-1938). He was selected to the Pro Bowl in 1938 and in 1982 was inducted into the Oregon Sports Hall of Fame. His home was in Astoria, Oregon.

Private First Class Joseph Pantillion Martinez

Private Joseph Pantillion Martinez was killed in action on May 26, 1943. He was 23 years old when he was killed. He was drafted into the Army in August 1942. He was one of nine children. On October 27, 1943, the War Department published General Order No. 71 awarding Private First Class Joseph P. Martinez the Medal of Honor, the only one for the North Pacific. The Medal of Honor is the United States highest military decoration. Private Joseph P. Martinez was buried with full military honors in his childhood home of Ault, Colorado. The military posthumously honored Martinez by naming a transport ship and military installation after him. Several municipalities erected statues in his honor as well.

Colonel Yasuyo Yamasaki

Colonel Yasuyo Yamasaki, often spelled Yamazaki (October 17, 1891 – May 29, 1943) was a Japanese Army Officer who commanded the Japanese forces on Attu during the Battle of Attu in World War II. Yamasaki was a native of what is now part of Tsuru, Yamanashi, where his father was a Buddhist priest. He arrived on Attu in April 1943 by submarine. The 2,650 defenders under Yamasaki did not contest the American landings on Attu, but rather dug in on high ground away from the shore. The battle produced some of the bloodiest fighting in the American Theater and the Pacific Theater, similar to the battles of Iwo Jima and Okinawa. On May 29, 1943 the last of the Japanese forces suddenly attacked near Massacre Bay in the first and only instance of a banzai charge on American soil. The charge was led by Yamasaki himself, who was killed later that day in the largest banzai charge in World War II.

The Medal of Honor was awarded posthumously to Private Joseph Pantillion Martinez – Company K, 3rd Battalion, 32nd Infantry, 7th Infantry division.

The Medal of Honor (MOH) is the United States Armed Forces' highest military decoration and is awarded to recognize American soldiers, sailors, marines, airmen, guardians and coast guardsmen who have distinguished themselves by acts of valor. The medal is normally awarded by the President of the United States who is the Commander in Chief of the Armed Forces.

The Medal of Honor has achieved prominence in American History like few other awards have. It's a symbol for the very values in recipients displayed in the moments that mattered, an honor bestowed upon only the most honorable. But before it garnered such distinction, it started as a simple idea from Iowa Senator James W. Grimes – a bill authorizing the production and distribution of “Medals of Honor” to be presented to enlisted seamen and marines who “distinguish themselves by gallantry in action and other seamen-like qualities” during the American Civil War. On December 21, 1861, President Abraham Lincoln signed the legislation creating the Navy's Medal of Honor.

The Distinguished Service Cross was awarded to Captain Delbert Leonard Bjork – Headquarters, U.S. Army Troops, APO 726 (Attu Landing Force), General Orders No. 31 (1943). Company F, 2nd Battalion, 17th Infantry, 7th Army Division.

The Distinguished Service Cross is the second highest military award that can be given to a member of the United States Army (and previously, the United States Army Air forces), for extreme gallantry and risk of life in actual combat with an armed enemy force. Actions that merit the Distinguished Service Cross must be of such a high degree that they are above those required for all other U.S. combat decorations but do not meet the criteria for the Medal of Honor. The Distinguished Service Cross is equivalent to the Navy Cross, Marine Corps Cross, Coast Guard Cross, and the Air Force Cross.

The Distinguished Service Cross was first awarded during World War I. In addition, a number of awards were made for actions before World War I. In many cases, these were to soldiers who had received a Certificate of Merit for gallantry which, at the time, was the only other honor for gallantry the Army could award, or recommend a Medal of Honor.

The Silver Star Medal was awarded posthumously to 1st Lieutenant Albert Paul Fong on August 27, 1943. Company F, 2nd Battalion, 17th Infantry, 7th Army Division.

The Silver Star Medal (SSM), or Silver Star, is the third highest military award for valorous actions in combat. The origins of the Silver Star date back to July 9, 1918, when a Congressional Act authorized the issuance of the "Silver Star for acts of gallantry against enemies of the United States," or while serving with friendly foreign forces "Engaged in armed conflict against an opposing armed force in which the United States is not a belligerent party." Furthermore, on August 7, 1942, Congress authorized the issuance of the Silver Star to non-military civilians for equal acts of gallantry against enemies of the United States. The Silver Star was the successor of the "Citation Star," issued by the Department of War during World War I, and its design reflects its specific lineage.

The Silver Star was designed by Rudolf Freund of Bailey, Banks and Biddle, a jeweler in Philadelphia, Pennsylvania. The medal is a five-pointed gold star with a laurel wreath in the body of the gold star with a smaller star centered on the medal. On the reverse of the star, the words "FOR GALLANTRY IN ACTION" in raised letters span across the back of the medal. The medal is suspended on a ribbon of red, white, and blue stripes.

The Purple Heart Medal was awarded to Captain Delbert Leonard Bjork, and posthumously to 1st Lieutenant Albert Paul Fong, and Private Joseph Pantillion Martinez.

The Purple Heart, the first U.S. military decoration, instituted by General George Washington in 1782 and awarded for bravery in action. Although this was the medal of honour of the Revolution, it seems to have been forgotten for about 150 years. The 200th anniversary of Washington's birth marked the revival of the award in February 22, 1932. The current purpose of the medal is as an award for those wounded or killed (awarded posthumously) in the service of their country. An Oak Leaf Cluster is granted to a member of the U.S. Army or Air Force who already has a Purple Heart, and a Gold Star is awarded to a member of the Navy, Marine Corps, or Coast Guard for the same purpose.

Perhaps one of the most beautifully designed of all U.S. decorations, the medal is a purple heart-shaped badge with bronze edges that depicts a profile relief bust of Washington in the uniform of a general in the Continental Army. The reverse side bears the inscription "For Military Merit" with the recipient's name below.

List of Officers of the 2nd and 3rd Battalions, 17th Infantry Regiment

KIA=Killed In Action

WIA=Wounded In Action

2nd Battalion, 17th Infantry Regiment
Maj Edward P. Smith. CO
Maj. Ealon H. Standeven, XO
Capt Paul F. Mackin, S-1
1/Lt Charles E. Hoagland, S-2
Capt Robert J, Edwards, S-3
1/Lt Paul S. Hunt, Transportation Officer
1/Lt Vernon C. Blichhfeldt, Anti-Tank Officer
2/Lt George M. Bradley, A&P Officer
2/Lt Robert D. Jones, Communications Officer

E Company
Capt William F. Staab, CO
1/Lt George E. Adams, XO
2/Lt William A. Beeston, Platoon Leader
2/Lt William E. Copeland, Platoon Leader
2/Lt Raymond F. Bradbury Platoon Leader
2/Lt William H. Beeston, Platoon Leader

F Company
Capt Delbert L. Bjork, CO
1/Lt Albert P. Fong XO, KIA 25 May
2/Lt Harold W. Hahn, Platoon Leader; WIA 19 May
2/Lt Donald K. Reynolds, Platoon Leader WIA 19 May
2/Lt Paul H. Brundage, Platoon Leader, KIA 21 May
2/Lt Charles K. Paulson, Platoon Leader
2/Lt John W. Edrington, Platoon Leader

G Company
Capt Raymond E. Jones, CO, WIA 16 May
1/Lt Robert L. Washnok X0
2/Lt Walter C. O'Niel, Platoon Leader
2/Lt Robert E. Little, Platoon Leader KIA 25 May
2/Lt Francis f. Crohan, Platoon Leader KIA 22 May
2/Lt Joseph S. Hunter; Platoon Leader

H Company
Capt John f. Womack, CO
1/Lt Roland A. Baumgartner X0
1/Lt Marvin A. Elliott, Platoon Leader 11-23 May
1Lt Winfred O. Chancellor Platoon Leader 11-14 May
2/Lt Lawrence Leney, Platoon Leader
2/Lt Harry T. Moore, Platoon Leader
2/Lt Samuel W. Clevesy, Platoon Leader, KIA 19 May

3rd Battalion, 17th Infantry Regiment
Maj. James R. Montague, CO, 11-18 May, SD with Port HQ U.S. Army 26 May-2 Jun
Maj. Jack K. Siddens, XO, 11-18 May, CO 19-29 May, KIA 29 May
Maj. Lee Wallace, XO 18-29 May, CO 30 May-2 June
1/Lt Eugene L. Mcgee, S-1, KIA 29 May
2/Lt Robert O. English, S-2,W1A30 May
Capt Earls W. Nelson, S-3, KIA 29 May
2/Lt James D. Neill, Assistant S-3

List of Officers, Attu Island, North Sea Garrison

Headquarter, 2nd Sector, North Sea Garrison
Colonel Yasuyo Yamasaki
Captain Jiro Tsuya
Captain Hiroyuki Numata
Captain (Quartermaster) Kyoji Toba
Captain (Medical) Tsuneaki Yamamoto
2nd Lt. Hidesaburo Kaimori

North Kuril Island Fortress Infantry Unit
Lt. Col. Hiroshi Yonekawa
1st Lt. Tomigoro Kodama
1st Lt. Atsushi Shibata
2nd Lt. (Quartermaster) Sokichi Nakayama
2nd Lt. (medical) Hiro Tsunazuka
1st Company
Captain Yoshizo Ishigaki
2nd Lt. Kiyoshi Imai
2nd Lt. Matsuyuki Koide

3rd Company
1st Lt. Akira Sato
2nd Lt. Kenryo Mikami
2nd Lt. Sabuor Komiya
2nd Lt. Toshiaki Saito

303rd Independent Infantry Battalion
Headquarters
Major Tokuji Watanabe
1st Lt. Yasuo Okazaki
1st Lt. Yutaka Dobayashi
2nd Lt. Nasa Fuji
2nd Lt. Koichi Furuta
2nd Lt. Kosaku Iwai
2nd Lt. Masai Yoshida

1 st Company
1st Lt. Toshio Hayashi
2nd Lt. Yonezo Odashima
2nd Lt. Yoshimasa Kimikobe
2nd Lt. Kiyoji Ono

2nd Company
1st Lt. Hitoshi Honna
1st Lt. Norio Omura
2nd Lt. Takio Abe
2nd Lt. Shigeru Moriyama

4th Company
1st Lt. Yutaka Goto
2nd Lt. Taneo Chiba
2nd Lt. Harutoyo Hoshino
2nd Lt. Fumio Maekawa

Machine Gun Company
1st Lt. Yu Kato
1st Lt. Origami Kakutani
1st Lt. Keiji Takewaki

303rd Infantry Gun Company
1st Lt. Tomoyoshi Hashiba
1st Lt. Seizo Uchimura

North Kuril Island Gun Company
1st Lt. Chigoto Wayama
2nd Lt. Keiji Nakajima
2nd Lt. Shiro Yoshida

24th Independent Antiaircraft Co.
1st Lt. Toshisuke Sotoyama
1st Lt. Yoshifumi Okamoto
2nd Lt. Chikahiro Abe
2nd Lt. Kenji Suzuki
2nd Lt. Eiji Urase
2nd Lt. Seiichiro Koda

6th Fortress Mountain Artillery
2nd Lt. Taira Endo
2nd Lt. Shigeharu Nagayama
2nd Lt. Toshiharu Ikushima

302nd Independent Engineer Co.
Captain Kinzo Ono
1st Lt. Shigekiyo Suzuki
2nd Lt. Chikara Mitani
2nd Lt. Takehisa Saito
2nd Lt. Hosei Nukina

Antiaircraft Artillery, 2nd Sector
Major Masashi Aoto
2nd Lt. Takao Yokoi

35th Independent Antiaircraft Co.
Captain Nobuo Souda
1st Lt. Jinaka Ishii
2nd Lt. Takaaki Komasaka
2nd Lt. Isao Yoshida

The Japanese Doctor Paul Nobuo Tatsuguchi

Paul Nobuo Tatsuguchi (1911-1943) was a surgeon in the Imperial Japanese Army during World War II. He was killed during the Battle of Attu Island on May 29, 1943. A devout Seventh-Day Adventist, Tatsuguchi studied medicine in California and was awarded a California medical license in 1938. He then married his childhood friend, Taeko Miyake who was studying in California. Even though Paul and Taeko loved the United States, they went back to their native country in 1939.

In 1941, Tatusguchi was conscripted into the Imperial Japanese Army and ordered to report to the First Imperial Guard Regiment as a private. Later he was sent to the IJA's medical school and promoted to sergeant major. After Japan declared war on the United States, Tatsuguchi was assigned back to the First Imperial Guard Regiment. Because the army was suspicious of his American background, they never promoted him to officer status. He was eventually assigned to the 5216 Detachment North Sea Defense Hospital on Attu Island.

When Tatsuguchi was drafted into the army, he kept a diary of important activities he deemed worthy to write about. It was no different when the Americans landed on Attu in May 11, 1943. His diary was the only Japanese document written by any of the Japanese soldiers or officers about their personal impression of how the battle was going from May 11th to May 29th when he was killed.

When his diary was found, it was examined by army intelligence for military secrets, but none were found. Instead the translated copies were released by the 7th Division to the soldiers who were fascinated by his diary of a Japanese army doctor who was a Christian and got his education and doctor's license in America. Soon translated copies of his diary were published in America and reported in newspapers and on television. Here are his entries from his diary during his duty on Attu Island.

May 11th - Carrier based planes flew over, fired at them. There is a low fog and the summit is clear. Evacuated to the summit. Air raids carried out frequently until 1000 (10:00 am). Heard loud noise. It is naval gun firing. Prepared battle equipment. INFORMATION – American transports, about 41, begin landing at Hokkai Misaki (probably Red Beach). Twenty boats landed at Massacre Bay. It seems that they are going to unload heavy equipment. DAYS ACTIVITIES – Air raid, naval gun firing and landing of American troops.

May 12th – U.S. forces landed at Shiba Dai (Holtz Bay) and Massacre Bay. The enemy has advance to the bottom of Missumi Yama from Shiba Dai. Have engaged them. On the other hand, Massacre Bay is defended by only one platoon, but upon the unexpected attack, the AA machine gun cannon was destroyed and we have withdrawn. In night attack we have captured twenty enemy rifles. There is tremendous mountain artillery firing. Approximately 15 patients came to the field hospital. The field hospital is attached to Area Engineer Unit.

May 13th – Our two submarines from Kiska assisted us have greatly damaged two enemy ships. The enemy has advance to the bottom of Missumi Yama. First Lt. Suyuki died by shots from rifle. Continuous flow of wounded in the field hospital. Took refuge in the trenches during daytime and took care of patients during the bombardment. Enemy strength must be a division. Our desperate defense is holding up well.

May 14th – Continuous flow of wounded in our field hospital caused by the fierce bombardment of enemy land and naval forces. The enemy has a great number of Negroes and Indians. The West Arm Units have withdrawn to near Shitagata-Dai in a raid. I was ordered to the West Arm but it was called off. Just lay down from fatigue in the barracks. Facial expression of the soldiers back from the West Arm is tense. They all went back to the firing line soon.

May 15th – If Shitigati Dai (Moore Ridge) is taken by the enemy the fate of Wast Arm is decided, so orders was given to destroy all the wounded soldiers by giving them shots in the arm and die painless. At the last minute there was an order from Headquarters Sector Unit to proceed to Chichagof Harbor by way of Umanose (Fish Hook Ridge).

May 16th – At night about 11:30 o'clock under cover of darkness I left the cave. Walked over muddy roads and steep hills of no-man's land. No matter how far or how much we went, we did not get over the pass. Was rather irritated in the fog by the thought of getting lost. Sat down after 30-40 steps would sleep dream and wake up, same thing over again.

May 17th – we had few wounded and had to carry them them on stretchers. They got frost-bitten feet, did not move after all the effort. Met Sector Commander Colonel Jamaki (Colonel Yamasaki). The pass is a straight line without any width and steep line toward Chichagof Harbor. Sitting on the rear and lifting feet I slid down very smoothly and changed direction with the sword. Lay down about 20 minutes after that, went down to Chichagof Harbor. After struggling all the time, had expended nine hours, for all this without leaving any patients. Open a new field hospital.

May 18th – At night there was phone call from sector unit hq. In some spots on the beach there are friendly float type planes waiting. Went to Attu Village church, felt like someone's home – some blankets were scattered around. Was told to translate a field order presumed to have been dropped by an enemy officer in Massacre Bay. Was ordered to evaluate a detailed map sketch which was in the possession of Capt. Robert I. Edward from Adj. Of. Col. Smith. Got tired and went to sleep. First Lt. Ujue is now in charge of translation.

May 19th – The hard fighting of our 303rd Battalion in Massacre Bay is fierce and it is to our advantage. Have captured enemy weapons and used them to fight enemy closing under fog. Five of our men and one medical NCO died. Heard that enemy pilots dropped several bombs near Omanose (Fish Hook Ridge). The enemy naval gun-firing near our hospital is fierce, stopping about 30 yard away.

May 20th – Was strafed when amputating a patient's arm. It is the first time since moving over to Chichagof Harbour that I went in an air raid shelter. Enemy plane is a Martin (mistaken for a Wildcat). Nervousness of our CO (probably Captain Yamato) is severe and he has said his last word to his officers and NCOs that he will die tomorrow – gave all his articles away. Hasty chap this fellow. The officers on the front are doing a fine job. Everyone who heard this became desperate and things became disorderly.

May 21st – At 0600 strafing killed one medical man. Okayaki wounded in right thigh and fractured arm. During night a mortar shell came awful close.

May 22nd – Seventeen friendly medium bombers destroyed a cruiser off shore. By naval gun firing, a hit was scored on the pillar pole of tent for patients and the tent gave in and two died instantly. From 0200 in the morning until 1600 stayed in fox holes. The day rations 1 go 5 shakar (1.5 pounds) nothing more. Everybody looked around for food and stole everything they could find.

May 23rd – It sleeted and was extremely cold. Stayed in Missumi Barracks alone. A great number of shells were dropped by Naval gunfire, rocks and mud fall over the roof. It fell down. In a fox hole about 50 yard away, Hayasaka, a medical man, died instantly by a piece of shrapnel through the heart.

May 24th – Naval gun firing, aerial bombardment, trench warfare, the worst is yet to come. The enemy is constructing a position. Bn. Commander died at Umanose (Fish Hook Ridge). They cannot accommodate their patients. It has been said that at Massacre Bay district, the road coming through sector unit headquarters is isolated. Am suffering from diarrhea and feel dizzy.

May 25th – By naval gun firing, it felt like the Missumi barracks blew up and things lit up tremendously. Consciousness becomes vague. One tent burn down by a hit from incendiary bombs. Strafing planes hit the next room, two hits from a 50 caliber shell, one stopped in the ceiling and the other penetrated. My room is an awful mess from sand and pebbles that have come from the roof. First Lt. from medical corps is wounded. There was a ceremony to grant the Imperial Edict. The last line of Umanose (Fish Hook Ridge) was broken through. No hope for reinforcements. Will die for the cause of Imperial Edict.

May 26th – Diarrhea broke out and continues steady, pains severe. Took everything in pills, morphine and opium, then everybody slept well. Strafing by planes. Roof broke through. There are less than 700 left from more than 3,500. wounded from coast defense units. Field hospital held post office. The rest are on the firing line.

May 27th – There is pound trench mortar, also AA gun. The company on the bottom of Attu Fuji had been completely annihilated except one. Rations for about two days, wonder if Commander Yenegami and some of the men are still living. Other companies have been completely annihilated except one or two. Three hundred and third battalion has been defeated. Yenegami is still holding Umanose (Fish Hook Ridge). Continuous cases of suicide. Half of the Sector Unit Hq was blown away with machine gun. Ate half fried thistle. It is the first time I have eaten something fresh in six months. It is a delicacy. Order from the Sector Commander to move the field hospital was called off.

May 28th – Paul Tatsuguchi's last entry - Today at 2000 (8:00 pm) o'clock we assembled in front of Hq. The field hospital took part too. The last assault is to be carried out. All the patients in the hospital were made to commit suicide. Only 33 years of living and I am to die here. I have no regrets. Bonsai to Emperor. I am grateful that I have beloved wife, who loved me to the last. Until we meet again, grant you God speed. Miseka

(Misako) who just became four years old will grow up unhindered. I felt sorry for you Fakiko (Mutsuko) born February this year and never will see your father. Well be good Matsue (brother). Goodby. The number participating in this attack is almost 1000 to take artillery positions. It seems like the enemy is expecting an all out attack tomorrow.

Paul Nobuo Tatsuguchi in his Imperial Army Uniform

Landmarks Named After Killed Americans

1. Addison Valley, Creek – Amus Addison
2. Austin Beach, Cove, Pass – Captain Emory Austin
3. Ballentine Creek – Kenneth Ballentine
4. Bassett Creek – Captain John Bassett
5. Brannon Ridge – Lieutenant Anthony Brannon
6. Brewer Peak – Luther Brewer
7. Clevesy Pass – Lieutenant Samuel W. Clevesy
8. Gilbert Ridge – Lieutenant Harry Gilbert
9. Henderson Ridge – Lieutenant Douglas Henderson
10. Jarmin Pass – Captain John E. Jarmin
11. Martinez Mountain – PFC Joe Martinez
12. Moore Ridge – Lieutenant Robert K. Moore
13. Prendergast Ridge – Lieutenant Joseph Prendergast
14. Siddens Valley – Major Jack Siddens
15. Simpson Peak – James Simpson
16. Taylor Peak - Carroll Taylor

Photos of the Battle of Attu Island

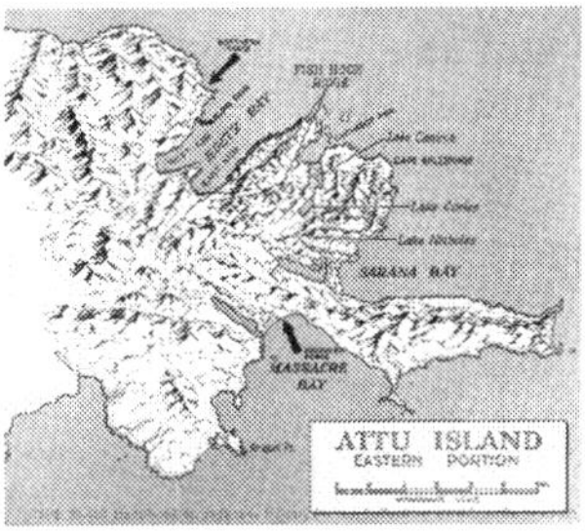

Attu Island

Attu Village

Americans firing a howitzer

Colonel Yamasaki & Officers

Japanese on Attu Island

American Supply Line

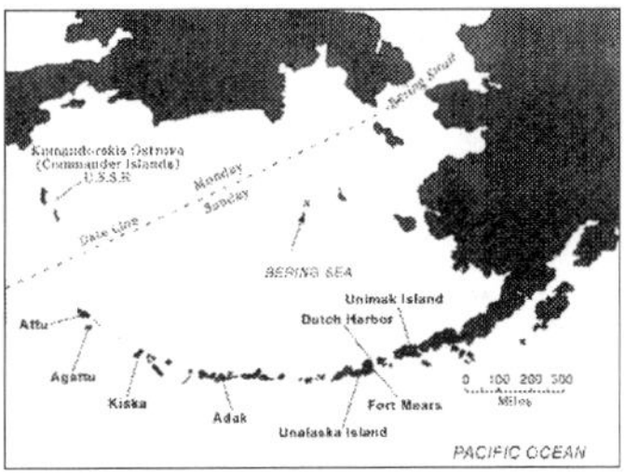

The Aleutian Islands

Injured Americans

More Photos of the Battle of Attu Island

Americans carrying a wounded soldier

Americans firing a mortar

Americans Landing on Attu

Americans pulling a heavy gun

Company F, 2nd Battalion,17th

Japanese on Attu -June 1942

Japanese Soldier

About the Author

Randall L. Got is a third generation American of Chinese heritage who grew up in the 1940s and 1950s in San Francisco, California. He served in the U.S. Army during the Vietnam War from 1967 to 1969 at Fort Polk, Louisiana when U.S. servicemen, that included the "Draftees," were unappreciated and ostracized for going to war that was being protested by the majority of Americans.

After his service in the U.S. Army was completed, he went onto a promising career in accounting and finance at CHA Industries and retired in 2004.

He is happily married to the same woman for 50 years and has three daughters and three grandchildren. He lives in Lake Oswego, Oregon, enjoying peace and serenity the best he can in spite of the never ending turmoil and conflicts in this world.

Bibliography

Chapter 1

Albert Paul Fong. Fold3 by Ancestry-Dennis V. Dupras, Pages 1, 3, 4
United States Army Training Center Infantry, Fort Polk, Louisiana, Company D, 1st Battalion, 1st Training Brigade, Pages 4, 5, 6, 7, 8

Chapter 2

7th Infantry division – Bing Images, Page 9
Fong Family Tree – Randall L. Got, Page 9
Sparks, Theresa A. - China Gold 1954, Page 10
Albert Paul Fong. Fold3 by Ancestry-Dennis V. Dupras, Page 12
Forbidden City U.S.A An Arthur Dong Film, Page 13
Fong Family, Historical Articles of Solano County online data base July 27, 2007 – Vallejo's Chinese Community Part Two: Into the 20th Century by James E. Kerns – Vallejo Times Page 13
H-History German General Erwin Rommel arrives in Africa, Page 14
Translate.com English to German, Page 15
Mojave Dessert- Wikipedia, Page 16
Attu the Forgotten Battle pg. 156, John Haile Cloe, Pages 16, 17

Chapter 3

Attack on Pearl Harbor–Wikipedia, Page 19
Time -Franklin Roosevelt Infamy Speech, Pages 19,20,21
H-History Germany declares war on the United States, Page 21

Chapter 4

Politifact- After Pearl Harbor, Page 22
National Army Museum – The struggle for North Africa, 1940-43. Page 24
The National WWII Museum-Battle of Midway, Pages 24, 25
Attu the Forgotten Battle pages 22, 23. 24, 31, 33, 36
John Haile Cloe, pages 25, 26, 27

Chapter 5

Attu the Forgotten Battle pages 39, 40 John Haile Cloe, pages 29, 30,

Chapter 6

Attu the Forgotten Battle page 40 John Haile Cloe, page 31
Japanese occupation of Attu -Wikipedia, Page 32
Attu the Forgotten Battle page 1 John Haile Cloe, pages 32
7th Infantry Division-Wikipedia, Pages 32, 33
U.S. Military Forum – Operation Landgrab, Page 33
Frigophobia – Wikiwand, Page 34
Attu the Forgotten Battle pages 47, 48 John Haile Cloe, pages 33, 34
Attu the Forgotten Battle page 156 John Haile Cloe, pages 35, 36
The Content Authority - Bushido vs Seppuku, Page 36
Britannica-What is the "Ides" of March? Page 37
H-History. The Rape of Nanking 1937 Page 38
National Archives – Executive Order 9066, Page 39
United States Holocaust Memorial Museum- Japanese American Relocation, Page 39

Forbidden City, The Golden Age of Chinese Nightclubs by Trina Robbins, pages 66 -75, Page 39
Britannica-Auschwitz Concentration Camp, Poland, Page 40
H-History-Operation Barbarossa, Page 41
Chicago Patterns -Trianon, “World's Most Beautiful Ballroom, Page 41
Albert Paul Fong. Fold3 by Ancestry-Dennis V. Dupras, Page 42
Wikipedia – M1918 Browning Automatic Rifle, BAR, Page 44
National Park Service – Battle of Attu: 60 Years Later. Page 44

Chapter 7

Attu the Forgotten Battle pages 46, 47, 48 John Haile Cloe, page 45
Attu the Forgotten Battle pages 66, 69 John Haile Cloe, page 46
Attu the Forgotten Battle pages 52, 65 John Haile Cloe, page 47, 48, 49

Chapter 8

Attu the Forgotten Battle pages 66, 69, 70, 72 John Haile Cloe, page 51, 54, 55, 56

Chapter 9

Albert Paul Fong. Fold3 by Ancestry-Dennis V. Dupras, Page 57
Wikipedia – Reverse Slope Defense, Page 59
Wikipedia – Pincer Movement, Page 60
Wikipedia – Bushido, Page 60

Attu the Forgotten Battle Pages 88, 89 John Haile Cloe, Page 61, 62, 63

Chapter 10

Attu the Forgotten Battle Pages 90, 91, 92, 96 John Haile Cloe, Pages 64, 65, 67, 68, 69
Attu the Forgotten Battle Pages 96 John Haile Cloe, Pages 70, 71
Attu the Forgotten Battle Pages 97 John Haile Cloe, Pages 72, 73
Jones, William S. Company G, 7th Infantry Regiment, 7th Army Division, Page 73, 74

Chapter 11

Attu the Forgotten Battle Pages 99 John Haile Cloe, Pages 75, 76
Attu the Forgotten Battle Pages 101 John Haile Cloe, Pages 77, 78, 79, 80

Chapter 12

Attu the Forgotten Battle Pages 102, 103 John Haile Cloe, Pages 81, 82, 83
Attu the Forgotten Battle Pages 104, John Haile Cloe, Page 84

Chapter 13

Attu the Forgotten Battle Pages 104, 105, 106, 107 John Haile Cloe, Page 87, 88
Attu the Forgotten Battle Pages 111, John Haile Cloe, Pages 90, 91

National Park Service. Battle of Attu: 60 Years Later
Page 90, 91
The National WWII Museum – Retaking the Aleutians
Pages 90, 91
Wikipedia – Pyrrhic Victory. Page 92
Attu the Forgotten Battle Page 173, John Haile Cloe,
Page 93
SOFREP- Military Grade Content, Pages 93, 94
National Defense University Press – Operation Cottage,
Pages 93, 94

Afterword

Photo Credits - William and Marian Got Pages 94, 95
The Hall of Valor Project. Delbert L. Bjork Page 96
U.S. Army home Page – Pvt. Joseph P. Martinez, Page 97
Wikiwand – Yasuyo Yamasaki, Page 97
Attu the Forgotten Battle Page 156, 167 John Haile Cloe,
Pages 98, 99
Attu the Forgotten Battle - John Haile Cloe, Diary of
Japanese Dr. Paul Nobuo Tatsuguchi Pages 100-106
Attu the Forgotten Battle Page 138-147 John Haile Cloe,
Pages 106
Microsoft Bing - Images of Battle of Attu Island,
Pages 107, 108
Cover Photo by Reddit – Piles of Dead Japanese
Medal of Honor – History and Time of the Medal of
Honor, page 100
Purple Heart – Britannia/Topic/ Purple Heart, page 103
Distinguished Service Cross – Military-history.
Fandom.com, Page 101
Medal of America.com – What is a Silver Star Medal?
Page 102